out of the moral MAZE

out of the
moral
MAZE
SETTING YOU FREE TO MAKE RIGHT CHOICES

Collegiate Workbook for Right From Wrong

Josh McDowell

Managing Writer
Dave Bellis

Writers
Bob Hostetler
Sam Douglass
David Howard
Karen Simons
Bill Colclough

World Bridge Press
127 Ninth Avenue, North
Nashville, Tennessee 37234

Distributed to the trade by Broadman and Holman Publishers

ISBN:0-8054-9832-X

Dewey Decimal Classification: 241
Subject Heading: CHRISTIAN ETHICS/TRUTH

Printed in the United States of America

World Bridge Press
127 Ninth Avenue, North
Nashville, Tennessee 37234

TABLE OF CONTENTS

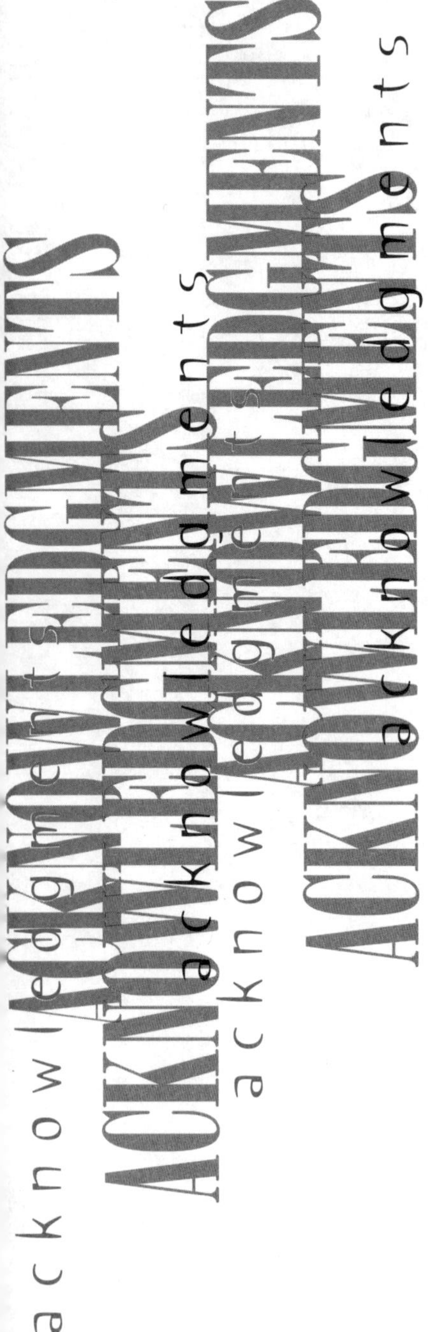

I want to thank and humbly acknowledge a number of people who brought this project together. If not for their vision, dedication, and talent, this workbook and the Teaching Helps in the back simply would not have been published. I acknowledge:

- Jimmy Draper, Gene Mims, and Chuck Wilson with the Baptist Sunday School Board, and Broadman & Holman for their vision and commitment to the Right From Wrong message and campaign.

- John Kramp for his skilled leadership, publishing vision for the Right From Wrong workbooks, and his untiring efforts as he championed this project on behalf of the publisher.

- Dave Bellis, my associate for 18 years, for directing every aspect of the Right From Wrong campaign, and being managing writer of this project, developing and focusing the content, and developing each product within the campaign into a coordinated package.

- Sam Douglass for his insights, unselfish devotion, and writing skills as he translated the Right From Wrong message into the workbook format. Also to David Howard, Karen Simons, and Bill Colclough for being a part of the collegiate team.

- Bob Hostetler for correlating and editing the Right From Wrong collegiate workbook outline and content into this workbook and for his witty and humorous writing style that brings a smile to every reader's face.

- Bill Colclough and Joyce McGregor for their insights and editing expertise as they readied the manuscript for publication.

Josh McDowell
Spring, 1995

Read this first!

Twenty years ago there was a short-lived game show in which pairs of contestants attempted to negotiate a maze in order to win the prize of their dreams. One partner perched high above the maze and shouted directions to the other partner who ran through the series of twisting walls, doors, and secret passageways. Of course, the one shouting the instructions had an unobstructed view of the whole maze; it was this contestant's job to determine the best way through the maze and to communicate directions loudly and quickly. The real excitement and fun of the game, for those watching on television, was to see the runner's confusion and frustration as he listened for clear signals and raced against a loudly ticking clock.

It's no fun being the one caught in the maze. Add the stress of the clock and the confusion of indecipherable directions, and you're in a real mess. That's exactly what many young adults are experiencing as they try to understand the myriad of messages they hear every day from professors, politicians, television personalities, parents, and friends. *Which messages are good? Which are true? Which way should I go? How can I find my way out of this confusion?*

The book you hold in your hand is a set of directions to help you determine the best way through the maze of conflicting messages so prevalent in our society today. This study is designed to restore biblical values and views for your generation. *Out of the Moral Maze* is an inductive, interactive workbook on a subject of great importance and urgency.

Out of the Moral Maze is designed to lead you on an eight-week journey out of confusion and into the clear light of God's absolute truth. Along the way, you may discover things you didn't know—things about truth, things about yourself, things about God. You may also discover that things you thought you believed or that you thought were true are not necessarily so. You may not like everything you discover, but you will find it challenging, thought-provoking, and ultimately, life-changing.

To get the most out of this workbook, set aside a specific time every day to study each day's assignment. Each assignment should take about 30 minutes. Take your time; don't jump ahead or try to complete several day's assignments in one day. Also, don't skip any assignments; each day builds on the next and each group of assignments are designed to complement each other.

This study is also designed to be used in connection with weekly group sessions that will help clarify or amplify your understanding of the concepts you learn in individual study. Be as faithful as possible to the group sessions and you will reap even greater reward from your personal study.

Beyond the group Bible study and the individual assignments, this study includes weekly case studies, "The Scene on Campus," which follows the journey of a freshman as she encounters differing systems of belief, different lifestyles, and difficult decisions about her own faith. If you are an upper classman, you will be able to relate and add to her experiences from those relevant to you. In addition, each unit includes five suggestions for applying the concepts studied during that week in different areas of your life. Try to do as many of the assignments in the Application of Truth as you can. The more involved you can become in this study of right choices the more you will gain in your own journey.

You're on the verge of a learning experience that could change your life and the lives of those around you. As you apply yourself to this material, may God apply the material to you.

How to Use Your Workbook

This study is designed for college students who want to find moral and spiritual direction in their lives, who are seeking guidance in making right choices in the major (and the everyday) moral decisions they will be making during the crucial college years. To gain the most from this study, you will need to do these things.

In Your Personal Study

1. For your daily study, you will need your workbook, a pencil, additional paper, and a Bible. Complete all written work on a daily basis.

2. Each week do the suggested assignments to help you begin to put into action what you've learned. These assignments are located in the Application of Truth.

3. Commit to learn the suggested Scriptures each week. Although memorization of Scripture is not a requirement of this study, learning the Bible verses which enhance the study will only amplify the message of God's truth in your life.

   Memorizing Scripture: Consider the following ideas to help you memorize Scripture.

   a. Read the verse and think about the meaning.

   b. Write the verse on notecards, one phrase per card.

   c. Glance at the first phrase and say it aloud. Glance at the next phrase and say both. Continue this process until you have said the whole phrase.

   d. Try to say the verse from memory later in the day. If you have trouble, glance at the cards.

   e. Repeat the verse several times each day for a week until you feel that the verse is firmly implanted in your mind.

4. Read Josh McDowell's book *Right From Wrong*. If your local bookstore does not carry it, ask them to order a copy for you. Use the ordering information on pp. 172-175.

In Preparation for Group Sessions

1. Attend all of the group sessions. You have probably received this workbook at the first group session. Each week you will need to do all of that week's activities and assignments before the next group session. This is your schedule.

Before Group Session	**Complete in your workbook**
Introductory Session	Overview and receive workbooks
1	Week 1: Absolute Truth
2	Week 2: An Acceptable Standard
3	Week 3: Precept/Principle/Person
4	Week 4: Discover the 4Cs
5	Week 5: Random Acts of Honesty
6	Week 6: Love Protection
7	Week 7: Handbook for Great Sex
8	Week 8: Directions for the Maze

2. Take your workbook to every group session along with pencil, paper, and your Bible. Your workbook includes the worksheets you will use during the group sessions.

3. Invite others to join you in this study.

They called it "Keeping Score."

Nineteen-year-old Billy Shehan claimed the lead in the game with 66 points. His closest competitor, 20 year-old Dana Belman, had scored 63 times. A basketball game? Card game? Archery?

No, they were playing sex.

Billy and Dana were members of the infamous Spur Posse, in Lakewood, California, a middle-class suburb of Los Angeles with cookie cutter houses and neatly-clipped lawns. The Spurs became famous when (after nine of them, ages 15 to 18, had been arrested on charges of rape and molestation) the media learned that they had devised a scoring system to keep track of their sexual conquests. The Spurs scored one point for each different girl they "hooked up [had sex] with."

Mike Weber, one of the most feared Spurs, explained the code the young adults used to communicate their latest score. "When somebody would be with a girl, he would say I'm [baseball player] Steve Sax [uniform number 7] or I'm [football player] Barry Sanders [uniform number 20]."

As the young adults tallies increased, so did accusations of intimidation and rape. One sixteen-year-old girl reported that a Spur removed her clothes during a sexual encounter in a park and refused to return them until she had sex with other Spurs; she believes she averted a gang rape by screaming until her clothes were returned. An 11 year-old girl said that she was sleeping over at a girlfriend's house when a boy sneaked into her bedroom window, apparently a common Spur practice, and told her he wanted to have sex with her. She complied, explaining later that she did so because she had heard that Spurs would hurt girls who didn't cooperate.

The young adults admitted that the girls they slept with were mere statistics. "It's got nothing to do with love," said 18 year-old Matt Nielsen. "It's got nothing to do with liking them." Indeed, the boys referred to their conquests as "whores" and "sluts." And none of the Spurs seemed embarrassed, much less remorseful about their conduct. "It was not a big deal," Mike Weber said, "If you had sex, you got a point. It was like bragging rights for the person who thought he was the biggest stud."

Incredible, isn't it? How could anyone think that such conduct is not a big deal? How could anyone seriously argue that such conduct is perfectly moral? How could anyone justify such actions with a shrug of the shoulder? Unfortunately, it happens all the time. And not just among the Spurs.

Revelations of widespread cheating at the U.S. Naval Academy resulted in eleven students being recommended for expulsion; some estimates claimed that as many of 125 students cheated on a final exam in electrical engineering. Many people stated that the students had done nothing wrong, they had simply made a mistake: they got caught.

Cornell University forced Christian residence hall assistants (R.A.s) to watch pornographic movies of hardcore gay and lesbian sex. Why? To make the R.A.s more "sensitive" to gay and lesbian issues and behaviors. Violent and immoral behavior at a large midwestern university became so bad that the board of regents attempted to institute codes of behavior, such as standards intended to prevent date rape and underage consumption of alcohol, to ensure a degree of civil behavior and personal safety. Several students dropped out to protest the proposed limits on their personal freedoms.

These are not isolated incidents. People all over this country share similar attitudes toward morality.

These people are all over the country, and all over our college campuses. They are men, and they are women; they are in dorms, apartments, fraternity and sorority houses; they participate on athletic and debate teams; they are white, black, Asian, native American, and Hispanic. What unites them is a belief that the line between right and wrong is different for everyone; they believe that truth is a matter of taste, and morality is nothing more than an individual's preference. They espouse a view of truth and morality that is commonly known as "relativism."

Relativism, according to Webster, is "a view that ethical truths depend on the individuals and groups holding them." Relativism is often expressed in the words, "Just because it's right for you doesn't mean it's right for me." Relativism is reflected in the objection, "You can't tell me what's right or wrong; I've got to decide that for myself!" Relativism has even been codified by the United States Supreme Court in Planned Parenthood v. Casey, in which the court declared that it is up to each individual to determine "the concept of existence, of meaning, of the universe, and of the mystery of human life."

To a relativist, morality is open to individual interpretation. Right and wrong are subject to change. Truth can be as fluid and changing as Heraclitus's river.[1] As a result, though there have always been "wild and rebellious kids who would go off the track and do something wrong,"[2] today's kids — as well as their parents, teachers, and government — don't even know where "the track" is. They're lost in a moral maze, victims (and perpetrators) of a crisis of truth.

This study will attempt to help you through the moral maze which confuses so much of contemporary society. We will:

1. Show how a person's views about truth affect his or her actions and attitudes.

2. Lead you on a search for an objective standard of right and wrong.

3. Look at teachings and examples from the Bible—both negative and positive—which illustrate the "absolute confusion" of today's society.

4. Provide a simple—but effective—tool to use when you face difficult moral decisions.

5. Equip you to take a stand in a culture that is intolerant of truth.

After the main teaching in each unit, there are several sections which will assist you in understanding these truths and putting them into practice.

- **The Scene on Campus** is a case study about the first semester in college for Cynthia Adams, a Christian freshman at State University.

- **The Group Bible Study** will allow you and a friend or a group from your church, dorm, or campus Christian organization to discuss a particular passage from the Bible and apply it to your lives.

- **Individual Bible Study Sessions** are designed for you to examine your own life in light of God's teachings.

- **The Application of Truth** will suggest five action tasks from which you can actively learn about and begin to incorporate the topic at hand.

During the next few weeks, start to become aware of your own beliefs and how you have been influenced in these beliefs. Many of the sidebars (quotes in the margins) come from within our culture—TV, music, movies, books, and others. Rather than simply allow these "influencers" (and others you encounter) to flow unhindered into your mind and your life, filter them; examine them; ask whether or not they are true. When you listen to music—even Christian music—or go to movies or watch TV or read books or hear a lecture, THINK about what you hear.

We do indeed live in a confusing culture at a confusing time. If you accept and practice the lessons within this book, you can lessen the confusion in your own life and decisions, and you can influence others around you to do the same.

Notes from absolute truth

1. I have the following questions...

2. I have the following concerns...

3. Because of the introduction, I feel...

CASE STUDY

Finally.

After an eternal summer of waiting for and dreaming about college, Cynthia watched her parents' Explorer, now relieved of all her worldly belongings, disappear down University Drive. She felt exhilaration, of course, but...also some apprehension.

She was close to her parents, closer than her sisters, probably because of the commitment she shared with them for their church. Cynthia could not remember not going to church; her friends teased her, saying that she had been coming to church nine months longer than she had been alive! During her senior year at Central most of them had been making plans to attend the Christian college two hours from home, but Cynthia's decision to come to State had been based on her major—Botany—and her family's finances. Private schools were expensive.

She found herself with a roommate she didn't know on a campus without her closest friends. Of course, she admitted, there was Jesse. She hadn't known him well in high school, only through his occasional visits to their Fellowship Christian Athletes meetings. Now, though, as the only familiar face among twenty thousand, he seemed like a best friend.

Jesse had stood aside as she told her parents good-bye. Now he walked up to her. "You wanna head to the orientation meeting?" he asked. Not trusting her voice, Cynthia just nodded.

Cynthia had met her orientation leaders—Matthew and Rosemarie—when she first arrived at the residence hall. They had even helped carry her clothes, stereo, and TV into her room! Matthew was a theater major and looked the part—tall, easily excited, a little talkative at times. Rosemarie was from Venezuela but had lost all trace of any accent. Her English was perfect; "better than mine," Jesse had noted.

Their orientation group was supposed to sit together for this opening meeting, and Cynthia was relieved to see Matthew motioning for them to join him and some of the others. They found a shady spot and settled in to hear an upperclassman introduce the Dean of Student Affairs, Dr. Prentice Marham. Dr. Marham received a warm welcome, especially from the orientation leaders. Matthew leaned over to Cynthia and Jesse and whispered, "Just about everybody loves Dr. Marham. She has only been here a couple of years and has made an incredible difference in the campus climate. Native Americans, Hispanics, and African-American students have been able to attain some very influential positions in Student Government Association—the racial climate has really smoothed out. Even the homophobes have pretty much disappeared!"

Cynthia looked curiously at Matthew but the Dean had begun speaking. "Welcome to State University! You have joined a proud heritage of individuals who have come to this place to get a degree and have left here with something different—an education! A new awareness of themselves and a new way of looking at the world around them! A new perspective! Many of you have come from a background where parents, teachers, or ministers have purported to tell you what's real and what's right. But you're in college, now. Here at State, there's no one to do your thinking for you—you will have to make your own decisions, form your own conclusions, follow your own inner voice. You are going to leave behind the racism, the anglocentrism, the homophobia, the heterosexism, the philosophies and theologies that have stunted your thinking." She tapped her temple with a long forefinger.

"Here at State we celebrate diversity; we promote the unusual; we champion the individual! You're not living at home anymore, men and women. You're free now; free to say whatever you want to say. Free to do whatever you want to do. Free to be whatever you want to be!"

The crowd of resident advisors and new students stood and roared their approval. Cynthia stood with them, and clapped like the rest. She had been moved by the address. But something—she wasn't sure what—bothered her.

"This would be the year we turned 18. We had waited a decade to vote, a decade to drink, a decade to go club hopping and to pack our bags to far-off reaches of higher education."

"Age 18 wasn't what we thought it would be," (USA Today, 12/27/94)

Questions:

1. How would you describe the belief system behind the Dean's address?

2. Have you encountered anyone on campus who shared this belief system? What has been the nature of these encounters?

3. Why was Cynthia disturbed by the address?

4. What would your thoughts have been if you had been a new student attending the orientation meeting?

?

CASE STUDY

BIBLE STUDY PASSAGE

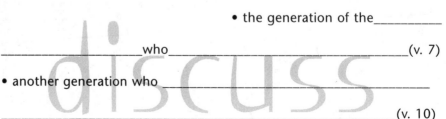

Do you think the United States is in a moral and spiritual decline?
76% Yes
20% No
The Newsweek Poll, June 2-3, 1994

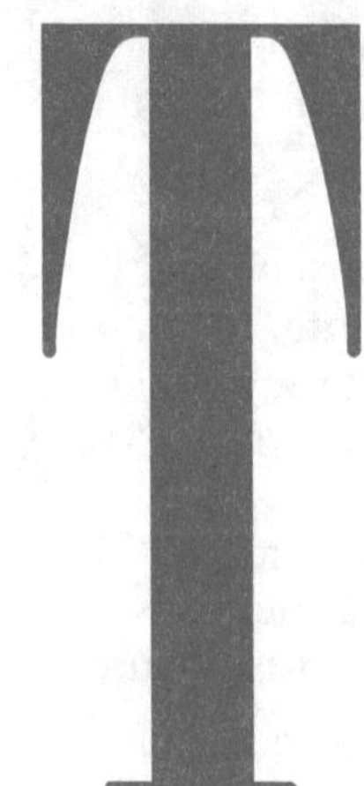

here once was a time when Americans grew up in a culture that communicated absolute standards for behavior: certain things were always right and certain things were always wrong. A child's parents, teachers, ministers, and other adults collaborated in an effort to communicate that the former should be practiced and the latter should be avoided. At one time, our society, by and large, explained the universe, humanity, and the purpose of life from the belief that absolute truth existed, and everyone could know and understand it. While, obviously, not everyone obeyed those guidelines, a clear understanding of what was right and wrong gave society a moral standard by which to measure crime and punishment, business ethics, community values, character, and social conduct. It became the lens through which society viewed law, science, the arts, and politics—the whole of culture. It provided a cohesive model that promoted the healthy development of the individual and the family, united communities, and encouraged personal responsibility and moral behavior. That has changed drastically, however. Our...society...has largely rejected the notions of truth and morality, [and has become] a society that has somewhere lost the ability to decide what is true and what is right (*Right From Wrong*, p. 13).

Contemporary Western society is not the first to make such a tragic and far-reaching mistake. This unit's group study will explore the effects of relativism on an earlier culture.

Judges 2:6-19

After Joshua had dismissed the Israelites, they went to take possession of the land, each to his own inheritance. The people served the LORD throughout the lifetime of Joshua and of the elders who outlived him and who had seen all the great things the LORD had done for Israel.

Joshua son of Nun, the servant of the LORD, died at the age of a hundred and ten. And they buried him in the land of his inheritance, at Timnath Heres in the hill country of Ephraim, north of Mount Gaash.

After that whole generation had been gathered to their fathers, another generation grew up, who knew neither the LORD nor what he had done for Israel. Then the Israelites did evil in the eyes of the LORD and served the Baals. They forsook the LORD, the God of their fathers, who had brought them out of Egypt. They followed and worshiped various gods of the peoples around them. They provoked the LORD to anger because they forsook him and served Baal and the Ashtoreths. In his anger against Israel the LORD handed them over to raiders who plundered them. He sold them to their enemies all around, whom they were no longer able to resist. Whenever Israel went out to fight, the hand of the LORD was against them to defeat them, just as he had sworn to them. They were in great distress.

Then the LORD raised up judges, who saved them out of the hands of these raiders. Yet they would not listen to their judges but prostituted themselves to other gods and worshiped them. Unlike their fathers, they quickly turned from the way in which their fathers had walked, the way of obedience to the LORD's commands. Whenever the LORD raised up a judge for them, he was with the judge and saved them out of the hands of their enemies as long as the judge lived; for the LORD had compassion on them as they groaned under those who oppressed and afflicted them. But when the judge died, the people returned to ways even more corrupt than those of their fathers, following other gods and serving and worshipping them. They refused to give up their evil practices and stubborn ways.

Read

As a group, carefully read Judges 2:6-19.

Discuss

1. Judges 2:6-10 mentions three generations. Can you identify them?

- those who lived during the life time of__________________ (v. 7)
- the generation of the__________ ____________________who____________________________(v. 7)
- another generation who ____(v. 10)

2. Can you remember anything about Joshua's generation, as described in the books of Exodus, Numbers, and Joshua? Share with the group.

3. What sorts of beliefs and behaviors characterized the third generation after the Exodus (vv. 11-19)?

discuss

4. Read the synopsis of that era of Israel's history in Judges 21:25. When everyone does "that which [is] right in his own eyes" (to use the King James Version's wording), what do you think will most likely characterize that society? (check all that apply)

- ❑ virtue
- ❑ anarchism
- ❑ relativism
- ❑ conflict
- ❑ unity
- ❑ security
- ❑ other___________
- ❑ socialism
- ❑ justice
- ❑ ignorance
- ❑ tolerance
- ❑ division
- ❑ wickedness

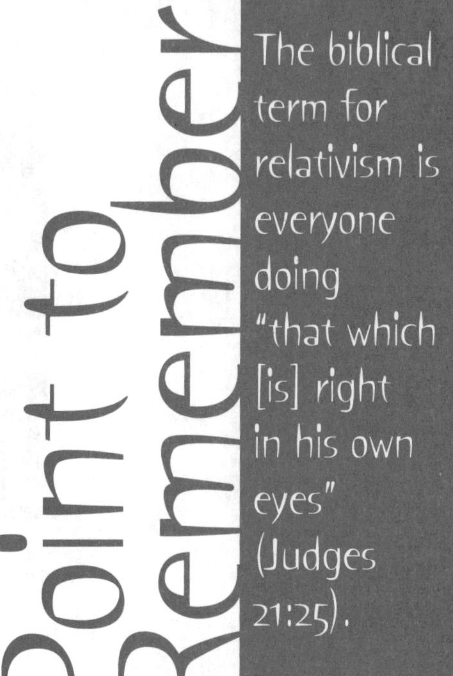

Point to Remember
The biblical term for relativism is everyone doing "that which [is] right in his own eyes" (Judges 21:25).

Today's Prayer

(Read Aloud) Dear Heavenly Father, as we embark upon this special journey through the "moral maze" together, please guide us by Your Spirit. As we study Your truths individually and as a group, help us stay focused and attentive to what You want us to learn. We come from diverse backgrounds and experiences, yet we have a common desire to know You better. Help us comprehend Your "big picture" of right and wrong, and help us conform to Your ways of truth. In the name of Jesus, who proclaimed that He is the Truth, we pray, Amen.

Discuss your answers with others in your group.

5. Do you think the description of that society (in Judges 2:11-19 and 21:25) bears any similarities to your culture? Discuss.

6. How do you think Dean Marham's orientation address (in "The Scene on Campus" section) relates to today's study? Discuss.

reflect

Reflect

1. To what degree are you different from the people described in Judges 21:25?

2. To what degree are you like them?

pray

Pray

Pray a sentence or two, expressing to God what you hope to achieve or accomplish in the coming weeks of this study.

Newsweek Poll

Who is to blame for the problems of low morals and personal character in the country? (Percent saying blame a lot)

77% Breakdown of the family
76% Individual themselves
67% Television and other popular entertainment
55% Government and political leaders
50% Economic conditions
44% The schools
26% Religious institutions

For this Newsweek Poll, Princeton Survey Research Associates interviewed 748 adults by telephone June 2-3, 1994. The margin of error is +/-4 percentage points. Some responses not shown. The Newsweek Poll © 1994 by Newsweek, Inc.

In your personal studies this week, you'll be looking at five facets of relativism from a biblical perspective. Each study will require you to read (and, if you like, make notes) in your own Bible. To explore the dawn of relativism, apply yourself to the following study.

Read

Carefully and thoughtfully read Genesis 3:1-24.

Understand

The traditional name of the first man, Adam, is based on the Hebrew words for "man." *Adam,* which is very similar to *adamah,* the word for "dust" or "dirt". The name Adam gave to his wife, Eve, means "living" (see Genesis 3:20).

Study

1. How did the serpent approach his temptation of Eve (v. 1,4)? Did he try to get the woman to (check all that apply):

- ❑ rebel against God
- ❑ doubt God's word
- ❑ deny God's existence
- ❑ reject God's authority
- ❑ distrust God's motives

2. Read Eve's response to Satan's question (v. 2,3). Compare her words with God's command in Gen. 2:16-17. Do you think Eve fully understood the command? Why or why not?

Verse to Remember

[the serpent said] "For God knows that when you eat of it your eyes will be opened, and you will be like God, knowing good and evil" (Genesis 3:5).

3. Was the serpent's promise to Eve in verse 5 true? Was it partly true? Explain your answer.

4. Which of the following collegiate characters do you think Eve was most like in her encounter with the serpent? (check one)

- ❑ bossy dean of students
- ❑ virtuous church-attending student
- ❑ dumb "jock" on campus
- ❑ the cheating student
- ❑ the student who doesn't "complain" about his activity of buying beer for everyone even though it's against his personal convictions

5. Do you think Eve was most tempted by (rate in order from 1 to 3):

_____the desire to taste the fruit
_____the beauty of the fruit
_____the chance to gain her own wisdom about good and evil, right and wrong

6. Was the serpent's temptation based on relativism ("you've got to decide what's right or wrong for *you*") or a conviction of absolute truth ("right and wrong exist independently of what you think")? Explain your answer.

Average number of violent acts per hour on Saturday-morning children's television: 22.8; percent of Saturday-morning programs containing violence: 94.7; percent of each episode of "Mighty Morphin Power Rangers" containing violence: 25.

"Breakthroughs: The Feats of 1994 That Have Changed Our Lives," (U.S/ News & World Report, December 26, 1994), 11.

Reflect

The relativist says, "Everyone must decide for himself (or herself) what's right or wrong." What is wrong with that view, logically speaking?

Today's Prayer

Heavenly Father, as I study Your Word, help me to diligently apply myself to it, help me to understand it, help me to apply it to my heart and life...and help me, having applied it, to obey it. In the name of Jesus, the Living Word, Amen.

Apply

What about you? Are your decisions most often based on relativism ("you've got to decide what's right or wrong for *you*") or absolute truth ("right and wrong exist independently of what you think")?

Pray

Spend a few moments in thoughtful meditationabout the above question, and then pray "Today's Prayer (on this page)."

Some of the fruits of relativism are apparent in the third chapter of Genesis. As a result of Eve's attempt to make her own decisions about what was right and what was wrong, she and Adam experienced guilt, shame, and punishment for the first time. To further explore the fruits of relativism, apply yourself to the following study.

Read

Carefully and thoughtfully read Genesis 4:1-16, the world's first account of sibling rivalry.

Understand

God asks four questions of Adam and Eve in Genesis 3 (vv. 9,11,13) and five questions of Cain in Genesis 4 (vv. 6-7,9-10). But God, of course, does not need to learn anything; His questions are used to increase their understanding, not His.

Study

1. This passage is remarkable not only for what it says, but also for what it doesn't say. For example, verse 1 explains the meaning of Cain's name; verse 2 doesn't explain what "Abel" means. Also, the order in which Cain and Abel's names are mentioned in verses 1-5 are alternated ("Cain...Abel...Abel...Cain," etc.). Why do you think the author of this account chose to alternate the names?

2. Verses 3-4 describe the offerings the brothers brought to God. Note the following about the offerings.

- Cain brought "*some* of the fruits of the soil"...but apparently not the firstfruits
- Abel brought "fat portions" (regarded as the best parts) from "some of the *firstborn* of his flock"

What do you think might be the significance of those contrasts?

3. Note that, according to verse 5, however, it was apparently not *just* the offerings that God accepted or rejected. The text mentions the man first, then the offering; God did not just reject Cain's offering, but "on Cain and his offering he did not look with favor."

4. What does God's statement to Cain in verse 7 imply? (check all that apply)

- ❑ Abel did not do right
- ❑ Cain did not do right
- ❑ Cain knew he was not doing right
- ❑ Cain's problem was inside himself
- ❑ Cain had trouble admitting the existence of right and wrong
- ❑ Cain was trying to make up his own rules
- ❑ Cain did not accept God's "version" of what was right

5. What was the outcome of Cain's relativistic attitude (vv. 8-16)?

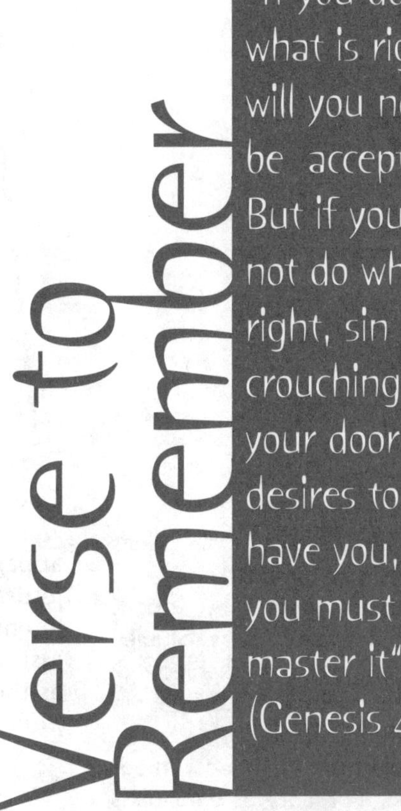

Reflect

Do you think a culture in which everyone makes his or her own decision about what things are right and what things are wrong will be (circle your choice in each pairing).

stronger	or	weaker?
peaceful	or	violent?
better	or	worse?
unified	or	divided?

Why did you answer as you did?

Today's Prayer

Father God, I submit to You and to the message of Your Word today. Please clear my mind through the ministry of Your Holy Spirit, and help me to see ways in which relativism has affected my thinking and my doing. Help me to see the fruits of relativistic thinking on those around me, that I might influence them, in Jesus' name, Amen.

Apply

Are you most like Abel or most like Cain? Do you ever have trouble admitting the existence of right and wrong? Do you ever try to make up your own rules? Do you (or anyone close to you) suffer the fruits of a relativistic way of thinking?

Pray

Prayerfully reread Genesis 4:1-16, allowing God's Holy Spirit to speak to you through His Word, and then pray "Today's Prayer" (on this page).

A relativist, to be consistent, would have to read the story of Cain and Abel in Genesis 4 and conclude that Cain did nothing wrong in killing his brother. His action may have been wrong for you or me, you see, but only Cain could decide if it was wrong for him. But, of course, most of us know better. We know that such a philosophical position is untenable. So, many people, unwilling to fully endorse the relativistic view of right and wrong, propose a *modified* relativism, which some call "cultural relativism." Cultural relativism says that a *culture* or *society* defines what is right and wrong for the people within that society.

Modernism. "The key assumptions of modernism is that knowledge is certain, objective, good, and obtainable," says Stanley Grenz, professor of theology at Carey and Regent Colleges in Vancouver, Canada.
Postmodernism. "In post modernism, the primary assumption is that truth is not rational or objective," continues Grenz. "In other words, the human intellect is not the only arbiter of truth. There are other ways of knowing, including one's emotions and intuition." In this relativistic environment, meaning depends on the perceiver, Truth is defined by each individual and the community of which he or she is a part.
"Reaching the First Post-Christian Generation." by Andres Tapia (Christianity Today, September 12, 1994), 20.

Understand

God called the prophet Jeremiah to prophesy to Judah when Assyria was the dominant world power and Judah was enjoying a period of apparent peace and security. God told Jeremiah to warn his people that Jerusalem would soon fall and its inhabitants would be taken captive. Jeremiah's message was greeted with skepticism and ridicule. Within just 40 years, however, God's words through Jeremiah saw fulfillment as the Babylonian empire rose to power and Nebuchadnezzar took Judah into captivity.

Read

Carefully and thoughtfully read Jeremiah 32:30-35, in which God details the offenses of the nation of Judah.

Study

1. God says, in verses 30 and 31, that the inhabitants of Jerusalem had provoked Him and "aroused [His] anger and wrath." How did they do that? (Circle T for true or F for false.)

T F They turned their backs on God
T F They skipped church on Sundays
T F They killed the prophets of God
T F They ignored God's commands
T F They set up idols in the Temple
T F They listened to godless music
T F They sacrificed children to other gods
T F They adopted the pagan practices of the cultures around them

2. According to verse 32, who does God say was involved in all the "evil" that was occurring in Israel and Judah?

3. What specific behavior made God most angry (vv. 34-35)?

"They set up ____________________."

"They built ______________________

____________________________to______________________________."

Verse to Remember

"They turned their backs to me and not their faces; though I taught them again and again, they would not listen or respond to discipline" (Jeremiah 32:33).

4. The behavior God denounced seemed to pervade the society of that day (involving the people, the priests, and the political leadership). What would the cultural relativist then have to say about those behaviors?

What did God say about those behaviors (v. 35b)?

5. Based on that passage, what do you think God would say about cultural relativism?

Reflect

If a person's culture dictates what things are right or wrong for him (or her), could anyone justly condemn the actions of the Nazis in World War II? American segregationists of the 1940s and 1950s? Proponents of apartheid in the 1980s?

reflect

Apply

How much do you let your culture decide what's right for you? Do you tolerate any behaviors that are "culturally acceptable" but morally questionable? Does your television or movie viewing reflect your culture's concepts of right and wrong? What about your language or dress? The music you listen to? Your habits?

apply

Pray

Pray "Today's Prayer" (on this page), meditating on how God may want you to respond to today's study.

pray

Today's Prayer

Mighty God, I praise You because You are the God of all living. Your love and Your commands transcend national, ethnic and cultural lines. I pray today that all who love You will listen and respond to You, even in the midst of resistant or rebellious cultures. In the name of Your Son, Amen.

Baby Buster Consultation cosponsored by InterVarsity Christian Fellowship and Leighton Ford Ministries pointed to 5 main characteristics that Xers are looking for in faith groups:
1. Authenticity. "We don't want no frills, no dog-and-pony show, no dancing-girls gospel," says twentysomething Piper Lowell, a Christian in the Washington, D.C., area. "What we want is unity, love, and acceptance."
2. Community. "I am homesick for the home I've never had" screams out the lead singer for the rock group Soul Asylum on their hit song "Homesick."
3. Lack of dogmatism. "Today an Xer, even if confronted with compelling evidence regarding the validity of Christianity, is likely to say, 'So what?"' says campus minister Jimmy Long.
4. Focus on the arts. "I'd rather be at a U2 concert than at church singing hymns," says Rudy Carrasco, 26, managing editor at the Hispanic Bilingual-Bicultural Ministries Association.
5. Diversity. For a generation seeking authenticity in a society and church notorious for its racial divisions, a racially diverse body of believers goes a long way toward authenticating the gospel.

"Reaching the First Post-Christian Generation." by Andres Tapia (Christianity Today, September 12, 1994), 20-23.

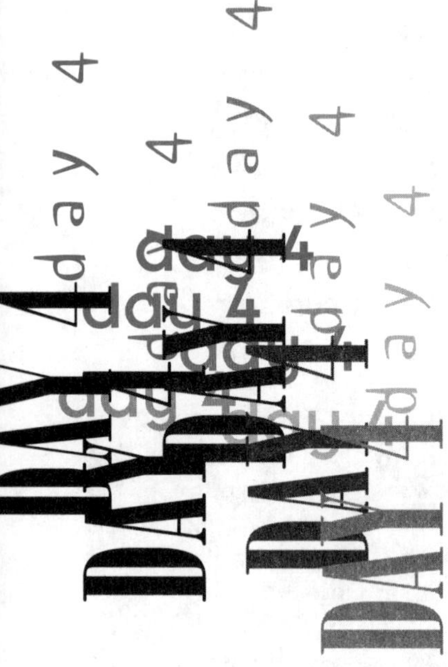

Another problem with cultural relativism is the problem of authority. A culture cannot exercise authority over moral decisions. A society cannot prescribe guidelines or exact punishment, because such a loose and changeful association of people lacks the consensus or power to conclusively decide issues of right and wrong. As Friedrich Nietzsche, the German philosopher, said, in the absence of absolutes, all that matters is the "will to power." In other words, in the absence of a true moral authority, might makes right.

Read

Read Exodus 1:1-22, the account of "the first holocaust."

Understand

The reference to a "new king" in Exodus 1:8 may refer to the passing of one dynasty (perhaps the Hyksos dynasty) and the rise of another.

Study

1. How did the Egyptian government in this account react to the growth of the Hebrew community (vv. 11-17)? (check all that apply)

- ❑ by enslaving them
- ❑ by negotiating with them
- ❑ by oppressing them ruthlessly
- ❑ by ordering the killing of all male infants
- ❑ by granting them equal rights

> Never doubt that a small group of thoughtful, committed citizens can change the world. Indeed, it's the only thing that ever has.
> — Margaret Mead
> *Utne Reader, Jan/Feb 1995*

2. How did the Hebrew midwives, Shiphrah and Puah, react to the king's order to kill all male infants born to Hebrew women (v. 17)? (check all that apply)

- ❑ by obeying
- ❑ by disobeying
- ❑ by resigning their positions
- ❑ by protesting

3. **IF** the relativist is correct, and everyone must decide for himself or herself what is right and what is wrong, whose action was right: the king, the midwives, neither, or both? Explain.

IF cultural relativism is correct, and a person's *culture* decides what is right and what is wrong, then whose action was right: the king, the midwives, neither, or both? Explain.

IF Nietzsche was correct, and the person or group with the greatest power decides what is right and what is wrong, then whose action was right: the king, the midwives, neither, or both? Explain.

5. Verses 20-21 imply a biblical answer as to which of the previous parties acted morally right. Reread those verses and write below who the Bible implies acted righteously.

Why do you think the Bible gives that impression?

Verse to Remember

"Blessed is he who has regard for the weak; the LORD delivers him in times of trouble" (Psalm 41:1).

Reflect

Do you understand how a view of "cultural relativism" could lead to the philosophy that "might makes right?" If not, review the introduction to today's study and evaluate each sentence individually.

Even relativists are uncomfortable with the full implications of their views; they don't want to admit that murder, rape, or oppression could be morally right. Why do you think that's the case?

reflect

Today's Prayer

God, I praise You because You are not only powerful, but You are righteous as well. Help me, through this study, to see issues of right and wrong through Your eyes, through Your Word, with the help of Your Spirit in my life, through Jesus Christ, my Lord and Savior, Amen.

Apply

How do you handle power? Does occupying a position of strength make you personally *less* likely or *more* likely to act morally right? Or does it have no effect? How can you counter the effects of power on your moral decisions? How can you ensure that you will make right choices even when you have the authority to make wrong choices?

apply

pray

Pray

Close your study time with "Today's Prayer" (on this page).

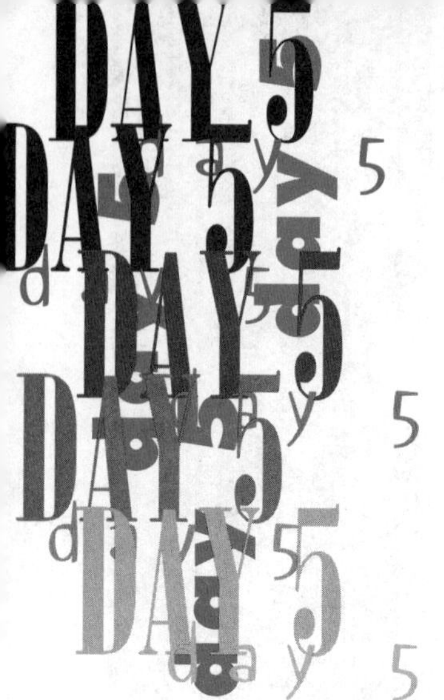

A leader in campus ministry has predicted that relativism, which for decades has enjoyed largely unquestioned acceptance among many academics and college students in our society, will soon be thoroughly discredited among thinking people. "It is so full of holes," he says, "that it won't survive...Christians need to have a voice in what replaces it, so they can influence it."[3] The greatest problem with relativism is that, taken to its logical conclusion, it will inevitably lead to anarchy — a state of lawlessness, a vacuum of authority. If everyone must decide what is right or wrong for himself (or herself), then no one — not even government — possesses the moral authority to question or proscribe an individual's moral decisions.

Read

Read Genesis 19:1-26, the story of an Old Testament "relativist's paradise."

Understand

In the Middle Eastern culture of Lot's day (and, to a lesser degree, in the present), hospitality to strangers was considered imperative (see, for example, Job 31:32). Lot's actions in this passage (some of which seem incredible to modern readers) are probably motivated by rigid adherence to this code.

> Little do we know
> "In moral and spiritual terms we are all sick and damaged, diseased and deformed, scarred and sore, lame and lopsided, to a far, far greater extent that we realize."
> *—J. I. Packer (as quoted in "Quick Quote" Current Thoughts & Trends, Vol. 11, No.1 January 1995, 7.)*

Study

1. Genesis 19:1-9 depicts the ultimate result of relativism: anarchy. In the absence of moral absolutes, nothing is forbidden, anything goes. Verses 4 and 5 depict one of the darkest scenes of Scripture. Consider the answers to the following questions:

- Was each person deciding what was right or wrong for himself?
  ❑ Yes ❑ No

- Were they acting according to what was acceptable in their culture (note that verse 4 says "all the men from every part of the city" participated)?
  ❑ Yes ❑ No

- Did the mob at Lot's door possess the power to force their concept of morality on Lot and his guests?
  ❑ Yes ❑ No

If the answer to any of the above questions was yes, a relativist would (in order to be consistent) have to assert that the actions of the mob were perfectly moral! Because the ultimate result of relativism is anarchy.

Verse to Remember

"There is a way that seems right to a man, but in the end it leads to death" (Proverbs 14:12).

2. How did the mob respond when Lot attempted to stop them from raping his guests (v. 9)? (Circle T for true or F for false.)

T F They became even more violent
T F They gave up and went home
T F They got angry at Lot for trying to "play the judge"
T F They complained to the block association
T F They tried to break down the door
T F They spit on Lot
T F They set fire to Lot's house

3. Why did the mob accuse Lot (in v. 9) of trying to "play the judge"?

4. How did God view the morality of Sodom, according to verse 13?

reflect

Reflect

Why is anarchy the logical result of relativism?

Today's Prayer

Almighty God, I praise You because You have planted in everyone, even those who do not acknowledge You, a basic awareness that right and wrong exist. I confess that, like Eve, I have often tried to pretend that I could determine right and wrong instead of seeking the truth. As I continue in this study, transform my belief and my behavior, through the power of the Risen Christ, my Lord, Amen.

apply

Apply

Have you ever been similarly accused of trying to "play the judge" when you objected to immoral behavior? If so, describe your experience below:

pray

Pray

Close your study time with "Today's Prayer" (on this page).

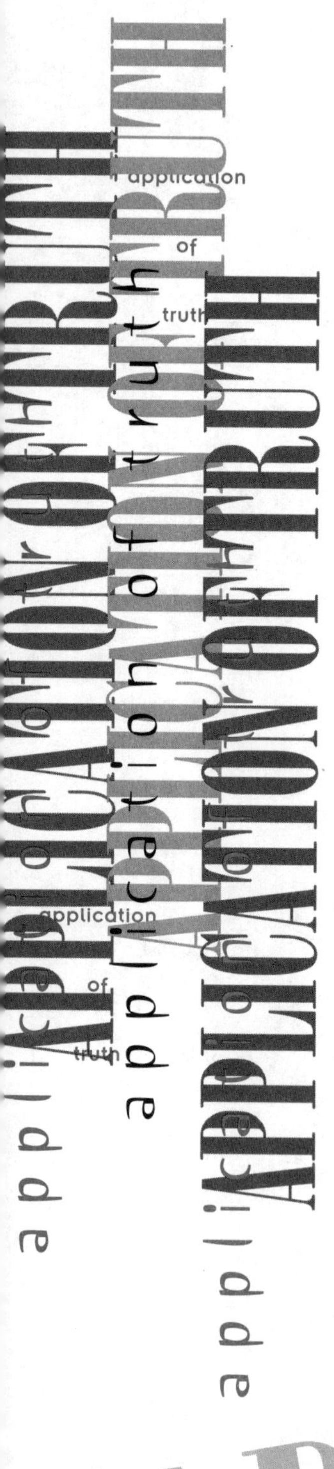

The Application of Truth section is intended to help you further explore the previous week's studies and take concrete steps toward expanding what you've learned and incorporating it into your life. You may not be able to accomplish all the tasks proposed each week, but you should try to do as many as possible.

• As you did in Day 1, evaluate the characters in the television shows and movies you watch: do they exhibit a belief in objective standards of right and wrong, or do they portray a relativistic view? Do they acknowledge any standard outside themselves, or do they do "that which is right in [their] own eyes?"

• Dean Marham (in "The Scene on Campus") suggested college life should be about "celebrating your diversity." Take your school handbook and look at all of the different groups and organizations. From a look at this list, what would an objective outsider say are the priorities on your campus? Is it spiritual life? How about cultural interaction? Social life? Ask four people, not just your best friends, what they think is "celebrated" on your campus, what priorities are reflected in campus activities and what forms of "diversity" are discouraged. How do those priorities differ from what you think is important? What can you do to influence the priorities on your campus?

• Observe closely the people around you (lobbies in the dorm are good places, as is the cafeteria and popular off-campus hangouts). Do your peers talk and act as if there is an acknowledged, universally recognized standard of right and wrong? Or do they truly speak and act as though everyone must decide what's right for himself or herself? Are their actions and opinions about right and wrong conscious or unconscious? Are they consistent or inconsistent?

• Make it a point this week to pursue statements about morality to their logical conclusion. For example, if a friend says, "Hey, I can't tell you what's right or wrong; you've got to decide that for yourself," you might pursue it like this:

1. OK, if that's true, then what if I decide that stealing your stereo system is right for *me*?

2. If you're to be logically consistent, you must agree that there would be nothing *wrong* with me stealing your stereo.

3. But if you say, "No, that would be wrong," then you're agreeing that there must be at least *some* standard of right and wrong apart from what I decide.

Get the idea? The more you learn to critically evaluate statements about morality, the more you'll incorporate this week's study into your life.

- Take note of instances when professing relativists assert their beliefs in absolute terms. For example, to a true relativist, tolerance is not a virtue unless the individual decides it's right for *him* (or her); yet many professing relativists promote tolerance as an absolute virtue. (It can be fun to hold relativists accountable by asking, when they make a statement that they consider true, "Is that true *absolutely*?" Be sure, however, that you do so humbly and kindly).

APPLICATION

[1] The Greek philosopher who used a flowing river to express his concept that all things in the universe are in a state of flux ("You could not step twice into the same rivers; for other waters are ever flowing on to you" [On The Universe, 483]).
[2] Roland Nethaway, "Missing Core Values," Cox News Service appearing in the Hamilton (OH) Journal-News, 3 November, 1993.
[3] Quoted in "When It's Wrong to Be Right," by Ginni Freshour, *InterVarsity* Magazine, Summer 1994, 6.

Notes from Session One

1. I have the following questions...

2. I have the following concerns...

3. Because of this session, I feel...

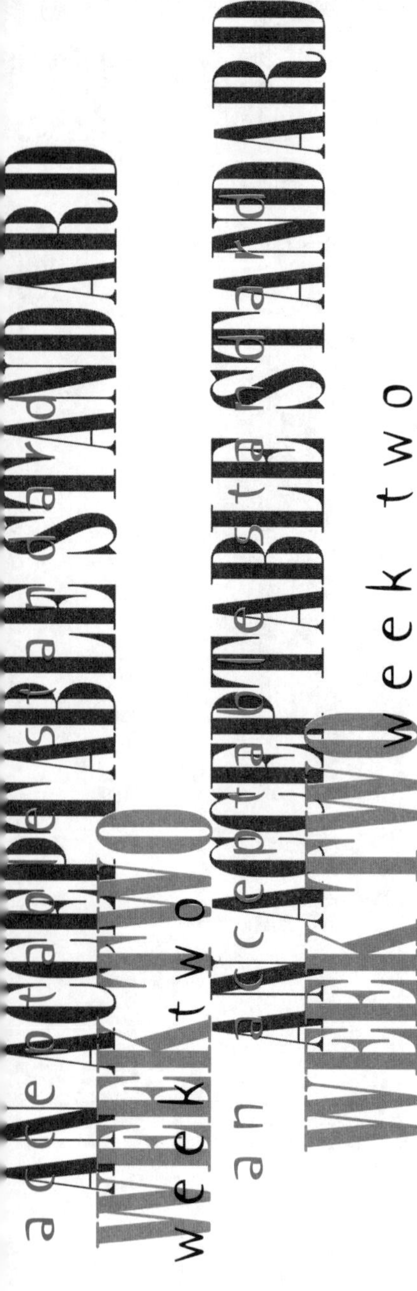

We all sense that something is happening to the moral foundations of our culture. What we're less sure about is why. What are the causes of the apparent moral crisis that afflicts our society, confuses us, and victimizes our friends?

Has young adult pregnancy increased over 500 percent in the past 30 years due to a lack of sex education? Has suicide among young people increased 300 percent in less than 30 years because we live in a more complex, stressful society?[1] Are violence, drive-by shootings, and guns in schools a result of ineffective gun-control laws? Or is there something more fundamental, more foundational at work?

Our craving for instant gratification and easy solutions will not help us here. We won't find an answer for adolescent violence at drive-through windows; a stop at a convenience store won't keep our classmates from lying and cheating; we cannot solve the AIDS epidemic in the space of a 60 minute television program. We must dig deep. We must look beyond the symptoms and deal with the fundamental root causes.

I believe that one of the prime reasons today's young adults are setting new records for dishonesty, disrespect, sexual promiscuity, violence, suicide, and other pathologies, is because they have lost their moral underpinnings; their foundational belief in morality and truth has been eroded.

A recent survey of young Americans revealed some startling information about their beliefs about right and wrong. The reactions to seven statements reveal that many hold very "flexible" concepts of morality.

- For example, only 43 percent of young adults involved in church say that an objective standard of truth exists. Though that percentage is not as high as among those not involved in church, it reveals that many Christians are likely to believe that "there is no such thing as absolute truth; people may define truth in contradictory ways and still be correct."

- More than 70 percent agreed with the statement: "When it comes to matters of morals and ethics, truth means different things to different people; no one can be absolutely positive they have the truth." This means that less than one in three believe that recognizable standards of right and wrong apply to everyone.

- Almost two-thirds (62 percent) agreed with the statement: "Nothing can be known for certain except the things that you experience in your life." Such matters as morality and ethics are up in the air.

CHICAGO — A 14-year old was indicted Wednesday on charges he killed a fellow gang member, an 11-year-old boy.
Derrick Hardaway was indicted as an adult in Cook county Circuit Court in the Sept. 1 shooting of Robert Sandifer, nicknamed "Yummy" because he loved cookies. Police said Robert was shot by fellow gang members angry over the attention focused on them after he allegedly killed a 14-year-old girl.
Houston Chronicle, 12/29/94, p.14a col 6.

• Among church-goers, 55 percent agreed with the statement, "Everything in life is negotiable." While it is doubtful that these individuals would really live their lives in such a way, it is disturbing to know that almost half would give intellectual assent to such a possibility.

For most people, however, the problem with truth is not believing that right and wrong exist, or even believing that it can be known. As Charles Sanders Peirce said, "Every man is fully satisfied that there is such a thing as truth, or he would not ask any question." The problem most people have is agreeing on an acceptable standard of truth. The greatest confusion in moral matters results, not from the question of what's right or wrong, but with the question, "Who says?"

"[There is] a growing degree of cynicism and sophistication in our society—a sense that all things are relative and that nothing is absolutely right or wrong."
—Jody Powell, former White House press secretary "A Nation of Liars," by Merrill McLoughlin with Jeffery L. Sheler and Gordon Witkin (U.S. News & World Report, 2/23/87)

Because they're unable to answer that question, many people get lost in the moral maze. They are confused about what truth is and who defines it; they are uncertain about what truths are absolute and what makes them absolute. In the absence of an acceptable standard outside themselves — by which to measure the rightness or the wrongness of their actions — many intelligent men and women succumb to the transient appeal of relativism. Whether they realize it or not, they make conditional decisions, choosing what seems to be the best alternative to them at the time, without reference to any fundamental or underlying principles to guide their behavior.

What is needed, then, is not only a conviction that relativism (the belief that each individual can — in fact, must — decide what is right or wrong) is a logically untenable position, but also an acceptable answer to the question, "Who says?" What we need is a suitable standard of truth.

THE SCENE ON CAMPUS

“So, what’s on your mind?”

The question ended Cynthia’s daydream. She looked up at Matthew with a brief smile of apology. The orientation crowd was moving in small groups toward the courtyard for dinner, and they were nearly alone in front of the stage.

She wasn’t sure how to answer. The other students had cheered Dean Marham’s eloquent welcome, and Cynthia admitted to herself that the speech was impressive. But she was uncomfortable, and she struggled to pin down the reason for her discomfort, like trying to capture a buzzing housefly in mid-air.

She finally managed a response to Matthew’s question. “I don’t know,” she said. “The Dean’s speech certainly gave me a lot to think about.”

“From the look on your face, you don’t seem to like what you’re thinking,” Matthew answered. He smiled patronizingly.

Cynthia straightened herself to her full height. “Well, I just don’t think I agree with everything she said.”

Matthew’s smile faded. “Oh, really? You don’t agree with people being empowered to make their own decisions? That was the founding principle of this country—freedom!”

“No, it isn’t that. I mean, I want to be able to make the choices that affect my future as much as you or anyone else does. That’s one reason I’m in college.”

Matthew seemed less defensive. “Then what’s the problem?”

Cynthia blinked. She opened and shut her mouth in several unsuccessful attempts to explain what was on her mind. She dropped her gaze. As she did, her eyes caught the glimmer of the gold cross she wore around her neck, and she remembered her pastor’s words to her on the last Sunday at home. He had stopped her in the hallway and congratulated her on the decision to attend State. “Where the night is darkest, the dawn shines brightest,” he had told her. “Go, and let the light of Christ shine through you there at State.” She wanted to do that; she just didn’t quite know how…Yet.

With resolve, she looked up at the young man. “Matthew, I’m a Christian. And some of the things Dean Marham was talking about just aren’t what I believe.” She prayed silently that Matthew wouldn’t press the issue any further; she wasn’t really sure *what* parts of the dean’s speech she disagreed with.

Matthew responded, “Cynthia, it’s cool that you have that kind of confidence. I respect that, I really do. You’ve chosen Christianity; and to you, that’s Truth. But you can’t say that that choice is right for everyone else. We all have to choose for ourselves, and that’s what Dean Marham was saying. You choose what you want to do, and I’ll choose what I want to do.”

Quickly Cynthia said, “Matt, I’m not trying to tell you what to do. I’m just saying…”

"Listen," Matthew interrupted. "I was raised thinking some of the same things you do. My parents would tell me one thing, my teachers and friends another, and the preacher still something else. And it was all contradictory. I stayed confused all the time. When I got here to State, I went to a program on self-actualization and finally started to think for myself. I realized that no one knows what's better for me than I do!"

He placed a hand on Cynthia's shoulder. "Look, Cynthia. For you, Christianity works; and that's cool. You feel free. For me, that's not where it happens. My world isn't black and white—it's not even gray! It's a rainbow of opportunities to live the way I want to live. You make your choices, and I'll make mine. What's wrong with that?"

At Iowa State University...on the opening day of classes last fall, requests for information or appointments with the student counseling service came in at the rate of one a minute.

Mel El fin with Andrea R. Wright, "America's Best Colleges," U.S. News, 26 September 1994, 86.

Questions

1. How would you contrast Matthew and Cynthia's views of Truth?

2. Matthew's beliefs can be termed "relativism." What is so compelling about these beliefs?

3. What is the deception behind that belief?

4. If you were in Cynthia's place, how would you have responded to the dean's address and to Matthew's remarks?

5. How would you answer Matthew's final question?

CASE STUDY

Hakuna Matata!
What a wonderful phrase
Hakuna Matata!
Ain't no passing craze
It means no worries
For the rest of your days
It's our problem-free philosophy
"Hakuna Matata"
music by Elton John,
lyrics by Tim Rice
©1994 Walt Disney
Music Company
(ASCAP)

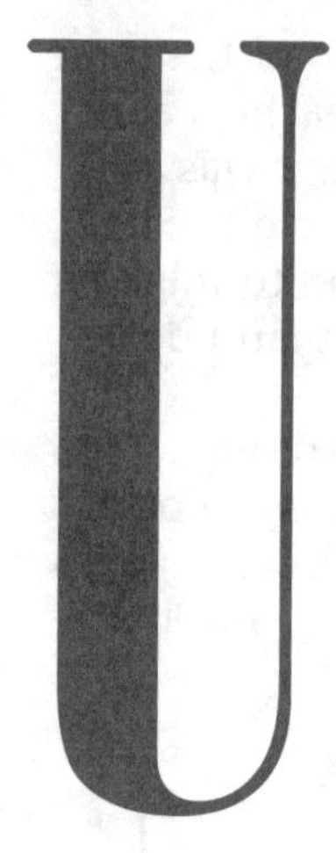

Ultimately, people hold one of two opinions regarding truth. Some people believe that all truth is relative, that the line between right and wrong is different for everyone. They believe that people may define truth in contradictory ways and still be correct. They believe that what is right for one person in a given situation might not be right for another person in the same situation. They believe that what was "wrong" for their parents' generation isn't necessarily wrong today.

Other people believe in absolute truth. That is, they believe that certain things are right for all people, for all times, for all places. They acknowledge that there are fundamental moral and ethical guidelines that exist independently of their personal opinion. They acknowledge that the distinction between right and wrong is objective (it is defined outside themselves — it is not subjectively determined), universal (it is for all people in all places — it does not change from person to person or place to place), and constant (it is for all times — it does not change from day to day).

Which position you hold will profoundly affect your behavior. If you believe that moral truth is relative, your beliefs and behavior will reflect that conviction. When you accept an objective standard for truth, you adopt a moral and ethical viewpoint that guides your choices of what is right and what is wrong. In either case, your "truth view" acts as a lens through which you see all of life and its many choices.

Genesis 3:1-21

Now the serpent was more crafty than any of the wild animals the LORD God had made. He said to the woman, "Did God really say, 'You must not eat from any tree in the garden'?"

The woman said to the serpent, "We may eat fruit from the trees in the garden, but God did say, 'You must not eat fruit from the tree that is in the middle of the garden, and you must not touch it, or you will die.'"

"You will not surely die," the serpent said to the woman. "For God knows that when you eat of it your eyes will be opened, and you will be like God, knowing good and evil." When the woman saw that the fruit of the tree was good for food and pleasing to the eye, and also desirable for gaining wisdom, she took some and ate it. She also gave some to her husband, who was with her, and he ate it. Then the eyes of both of them were opened, and they realized they were naked; so they sewed fig leaves together and made coverings for themselves.

Then the man and his wife heard the sound of the LORD God as he was walking in the garden in the cool of the day, and they hid from the LORD God among the trees of the garden. But the LORD God called to the man, "Where are you?"

He answered, "I heard you in the garden, and I was afraid because I was naked; so I hid."

And he said, "Who told you that you were naked? Have you eaten from the tree from which I commanded you not to eat?"

The man said, "The woman you put here with me—she gave me some fruit from the tree, and I ate it."

Then the LORD God said to the woman, "What is this you have done?"

The woman said, "The serpent deceived me, and I ate."

So the LORD God said to the serpent, "Because you have done this, "Cursed are you above all the livestock and all the wild animals! You will crawl on your belly and you will eat dust all the days of your life. And I will put enmity between you and the woman, and between your offspring and hers; he will crush your head, and you will strike his heel."

To the woman he said, "I will greatly increase your pains in childbearing; with pain you will give birth to children. Your desire will be for your husband, and he will rule over you."

To Adam he said, "Because you listened to your wife and ate from the tree about which I commanded you, 'You must not eat of it,' cursed is the ground because of you; through painful toil you will eat of it all the days of your life. It will produce thorns and thistles for you, and you will eat the plants of the field. By the sweat of your brow you will eat your food until you return to the ground, since from it you were taken; for dust you are and to dust you will return."

Adam named his wife Eve, because she would become the mother of all the living. LORD God made garments of skin for Adam and his wife and clothed them.

Point to Remember

The alternative to relativism is the belief in absolute truth; that is, truth that is "for all people, for all places, for all times."

read

Read
As a group, carefully read Genesis 3:1-21.

discuss

Discuss
1. What do you recall from your study of this passage in your personal Bible study experience this past week?

2. Imagine Genesis 3:1-21 as a stage play.
- Who are the characters in the play? (List them below)

_______________ _______________
_______________ _______________

- What actor would you choose to play each part?
- How would you separate this play into acts?
- Would you characterize it as a tragedy, history, or comedy?

3. Would you label any of the above characters as a believer in absolute truth? Would you label any as a relativist? Discuss.

4. Do you see any parallels between the drama in Genesis 3:1-21 and Cynthia's experience in "The Scene On Campus?" Discuss.

reflect

Reflect
1. Are you struggling to understand or articulate your "truth view?"

2. Look at the scale below; without actually making a mark, think about what location on the line would depict your current view of truth.

truth is relative — truth is absolute

3. If your position on the scale is not at the extreme right, what reservations or obstacles keep you from believing that certain things are right for all people, for all places, and for all times?

Today's Prayer

(Pray silently) Father in Heaven, we pray today for those of us who are confused about what we've studied so far; we ask You to clear our minds and aid our understanding. We pray for those of us who are resistant to Your truth; show us why we are often unwilling to hear You, and help us to heed what You say to us in this time together and in the coming week. We pray for those of us who understand Your truth, but have trouble obeying it; help us to join our behavior to our belief. In Jesus' name, Amen.

pray

Pray
Spend a few moments in silent prayer, as your group leader guides you to:
- pray for God's wisdom and guidance in thinking your way through these "truth matters"
- pray for the person sitting to your left
- pray for the person sitting to your right
- present to God any special requests or burdens you have about this coming week

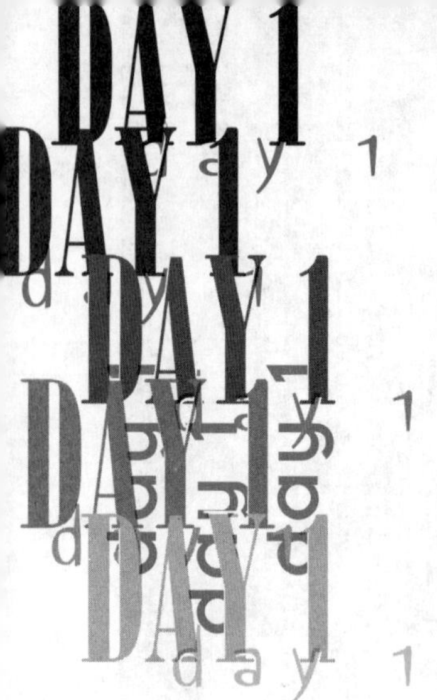

This week's studies will lead you through a search for an acceptable standard of truth. After all, even if a person admits that certain things are right for all people, for all places, and for all times, that still doesn't solve the problem of what — or who — defines what those things are.

Our problem at this stage is similar to a group of would-be baseball players who agree that correct measurements for a baseball diamond exist... but no one is sure what the distance between the bases ought to be.

Or, to put it another way, we are in a predicament similar to two cooks trying to bake a cake who acknowledge that the success of their efforts depends upon specific quantities of their ingredients... without a clue as to the right measurements of flour, sugar, and water.

So what do we do? We must search for an acceptable standard of absolute truth... some standard by which to measure the rightness or wrongness of certain attitudes or actions. Today's study explores the first qualification of an acceptable standard.

A recent Louis Harris poll for the Girl Scouts asked 5,000 American students where they would look to find the greatest authority in matters of truth. Where would they turn for that sense of authority? The answers that came back are very interesting. At the bottom are the media and the sciences. A few percentage points higher come parents and religion. Can you guess what the bulk of those students say is the greatest authority in matters of truth? "Me." The student himself or herself.

"Ethics: A Matter of Survival," by Rushworth M. Kidder (The Futurist, March/April 1992)

Think Thru

1. What kind of standards do people use for making decisions about right and wrong? What sorts of yardsticks do they use to figure out whether a certain attitude or action is moral? Circle any of the following standards by which you have seen (or heard) people define or defend the rightness of their conduct:

what parents say — public opinion — the law — conscience — what friends say — family traditions — a favorite teacher — horoscope — what others do — a pastor — culture

think thru

2. Have you relied on any of the above things to guide you in moral decisions? If so, underline those that you have used as a moral standard.

Verse to Remember

"There is a way that seems right to a man, but in the end it leads to death" (Proverbs 14:12).

3. Do you consider any of the above to be acceptable standards?

❑ Yes ❑ No ❑ Maybe

Why or why not?

read

Read

Carefully and thoughtfully read Exodus 2:1-12.

Understand

Though Moses had been raised as an Egyptian in the household of Pharoah (since he had been weaned; see v. 10), his Hebrew identity would have been obvious, not only to him, but to others (note v. 6).

Study

1. What choice(s) did Moses make as a young man (see vv. 11-12)? (Check any that apply)

- ❑ to go to bed with Potiphar's wife
- ❑ to intervene in a racially motivated assault
- ❑ to sacrifice his only son
- ❑ to worship pagan gods
- ❑ to kill an Egyptian
- ❑ to cheat on a freshman composition
- ❑ to hide the corpse of a murder victim

A recent survey reported in the Boston Globe says that 75 percent of all high school students admit to cheating; for college students the figure is 50%. A U.S. News and World Report survey asked college-age students if they would steal from an employer. Thirty-four percent said they would. Of people forty-five and over, 6 percent responded in the affirmative.

"Teaching the virtues," by Christian Hoff Sommers (The Public Interest, Spring 1993)

Today's Prayer

Father God, help me to study diligently, to listen attentively, to think clearly, and to respond honestly to Your Word in these moments. In the name of Jesus, Your Son, my Savior, I pray, Amen.

2. Do you think Moses used an *objective* standard (that is, a standard that existed outside of his own thoughts or feelings) to measure the rightness or wrongness of his actions?

❑ Yes ❑ No

3. Explain your answer below.

Reflect

- Do you think a moral standard, in order to be acceptable, must be objective? Why or why not?

- Do you think that's the only criterion for an acceptable standard of truth? Why or why not?

Apply

- Look back at the standards in the list above which you underlined (to indicate which you have used as a moral standard); are they objective or subjective?

- Do you always use objective standards to measure the rightness or wrongness of your beliefs or behaviors, or do you sometimes find yourself making Moses' mistake of letting subjective feelings or thoughts dictate your behavior?

Pray

Spend a few moments in thoughtful meditation and prayer about the above question, and then pray "Today's Prayer" (on this page).

A true standard of right and wrong must be objective; that is, it must exist independently of what you or any other person thinks or feels. Otherwise, right and wrong could change from person to person, in which case, though you may consider stealing to be wrong, you have no basis on which to inform your ex-sweetheart that it's wrong to swipe your large-screen T.V. with wrap-around sound. In the absence of an objective standard of right and wrong, your ex-sweetie may simply shrug off such behavior as wrong for you... but not for him (or her).

But there are many objective standards of behavior that are nonetheless unacceptable. The law, for example, exists independently of your thoughts and feelings, but it is not always an accurate gauge of right and wrong. Witness the laws of Nazi Germany, for example, or of South Africa before the abolition of apartheid, or of pre-Civil War America.

So, a true standard of right and wrong must be objective; but it must possess another characteristic as well.

Read

Carefully and thoughtfully read Exodus 2:11-15.

Understand

The word, "Pharoah," which appears throughout the book of Exodus (and elsewhere in the Old Testament) was a title, not a person's name. It was the Egyptian equivalent of "King," "Shah," or "Emperor."

Study

1. How did the situation Moses observes in verse 13 differ from the situation in verse 11?

2. How did Moses respond differently to the situation in verse 13? (Circle T for true or F for false.)

T F He called the police
T F He intervened with words instead of violence
T F He killed both participants in the fight
T F He tried to understand the situation
T F He ignored it

3. Note that verse 13 indicates that Moses concluded that one of the combatants was "in the wrong." How might he have done that? (Note: the text doesn't say.)

4. Verses 11-15 reveal that Moses believed in a moral standard that: (check all that apply)

- ❑ applied to the Egyptian assailant (v. 11)
- ❑ applied to the Hebrew combatants (v. 13)
- ❑ applied to himself (v. 14)

5. Do you think Moses' standard of right and wrong was universal (that is, applying to everyone, including himself)?
❑ Yes ❑ No

If so, then why do you think he judged the Hebrew (v. 13) for acting less violently than he himself had done?

If not, then why do you think he expected the Hebrew to conform to Moses' concept of right and wrong?

Verse to Remember

"He who conceals his sins does not prosper, but whoever confesses and renounces them finds mercy" (Proverbs 28:13).

reflect

Reflect

• How did Moses' "truth view" affect his behavior? How did it affect his future?

• Why must an acceptable standard of truth be *universal* (that is, applying to all people in all places)?

Today's Prayer

Almighty God, I know that You are all-seeing and all-knowing; I can hide nothing from You. Open my eyes to the ways in which
I try to conceal my sins,
justify my actions,
excuse my attitudes,
and get my own way.
Help me to confess and renounce my wrong attitudes and actions, and find mercy, through Your Son, Jesus Christ, Amen.

apply

Apply

• Do you ever apply standards to others that you don't apply to yourself? Do you demand behavior from others that you don't demand from yourself?

• How has your "truth view" affected your behavior? Your future?

pray

Pray

Thoughtfully read the "Verse to Remember" and then pray "Today's Prayer" (on this page).

An absolute standard of right and wrong must be objective and universal; it must exist independently of what you think or feel, and it must apply to all people in all places. Otherwise, right and wrong could change from one culture to another, or even from one community to another.

For example, you may consider it wrong to abuse children. In the absence of a universal standard of right and wrong, you have no basis on which to inform a neighboring culture or family that it is wrong to treat their children — or yours — in despicable ways.

But there is yet one more component of an acceptable, absolute standard of truth.

Read

Carefully and thoughtfully read Exodus 2:15-25.

Understand

The land of Midian, to which Moses fled, was located in the southeast portion of the Sinai Peninsula, and would have involved a journey of approximately two hundred miles. To someone like Moses, who was born and raised in Egypt, it represented the farthest distance one could go without encountering "enemy" armies.

Study

1. Notice that in verse 19, the daughters of Reuel identify Moses as an Egyptian. Why do you think they identified him as an Egyptian and not as a Hebrew? (check any that apply)

- ❑ they had never seen a Hebrew
- ❑ he was dressed as an Egyptian
- ❑ he spoke like an Egyptian
- ❑ he walked like an Egyptian
- ❑ he wanted to keep his Hebrew identity a secret
- ❑ his hair and eyes were adorned in the Egyptian fashion
- ❑ they knew their dad liked Egyptians better than Hebrews

2. Why do you think Moses came to the defense of the daughters of Reuel (vv. 16-17)?

Verse to Remember

"God... remembered his covenant with Abraham, with Isaac and with Jacob" (Exodus 2:24).

3. Verse 23 says, "During that long period, the king of Egypt died." In other words, Moses' crime had happened a long time ago, and the man who had sought to punish him was no longer living. Why, then, didn't he return? (check any that apply)

- ❑ he had adopted Midian as his new home
- ❑ the passage of time had not affected the wrongness of his crime
- ❑ he couldn't afford a bus ticket
- ❑ his wife didn't like to travel
- ❑ he didn't know whether the new Pharoah would forgive him or behead him

4. Do you think Moses could have convincingly defended his murder of the Egyptian by saying that it took place in another time, in his youth, during the reign of another king, in another land?

❑ Yes ❑ No

Why or why not?

I too have been teaching applied ethics course for several years. Yet my enthusiasm tapered off when I saw how the students reacted. I was especially disturbed by comments students made again and again on the course evaluation forms: "I learned there was no such thing as right or wrong, just good or bad arguments." Or: "I learned there is no such thing as morality."

...In teaching ethics, one thing should be made central and prominent: Right and wrong do exist. This should be laid down as uncontroversial lest one leaves and altogether false impression that everything is up for grabs.

"Teaching the virtues," by Christian Hoff Sommers (The Public Interest, Spring 1993)

reflect

Reflect

• Note that verse 24 says that "God heard (the Israelites') groaning and he remembered his covenant with Abraham, with Isaac and with Jacob." Those people had all lived many generations before Moses; God made those promises long before Moses was born. Why did God still consider that covenant important, after all those years?

• Do you think right or wrong can change from day to day, from generation to generation?

• Why must an acceptable standard of truth be *constant* (that is, valid for all times)?

apply

Apply

• Now that you are in college, and have started a new chapter in your life, are you ever tempted to call some things right that you once labeled as wrong? If so, why?

Today's Prayer

Eternal God, I am often changing. My attitudes change, my moods change, my beliefs change...But You are unchanging. Your throne endures from generation to generation (Lamentations 5:19); Your dominion endures from generation to generation (Daniel 4:3); Your kingdom endures from generation to generation (Daniel 4:34). Help me not to rely on my shifting opinions and ideas for moral guidance, but to look to You and to Your Word, in the name of Jesus, who is "the same yesterday and today and forever" (Hebrews 13:9). Amen.

pray

Pray

Pray "Today's Prayer" (on this page).

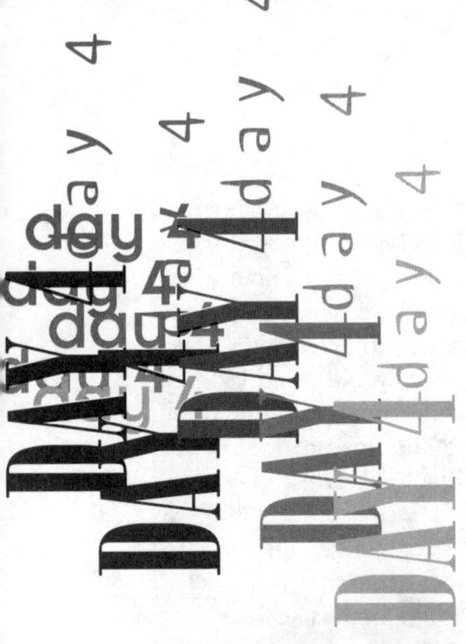

Absolute truth reflects a standard of right and wrong that is objective, universal, and constant; it is for all people, for all places, for all times.

This only makes sense, of course. If true standards of right and wrong exist, they cannot be personal, subjective, and fluid (or they are not standards, but simply opinion); they must be universal, objective, and constant. If they are not objective, then they may differ from person to person (in which case none of us has any grounds on which to dispute another individual's assertion that rape or racism is perfectly moral). If they are not universal, then they may change with circumstances (in which case none of us could maintain that child abuse and domestic violence are wrong in every case). If they are not constant, then they may change from generation to generation, or even from day to day (in which case none of us can condemn the atrocities of the Holocaust or the Spanish Inquisition, because they occurred in another time, nor can we reasonably expect to teach our children or grandchildren what things ought to be right in *their* time).

So where do we find such a standard? Our consciences? Our parents? Our pastors?

Although many students admit that cheating is morally wrong, they rarely report another student's cheating.

"Academic Dishonesty Among College Students," by Sheilah Maramark and Mindi Barth Maline (Issues in Education, August 1993)

Think Thru

1. Complete the following chart, placing a check mark under those characteristics possessed by each of the following "potential" standards of truth:

	objective	**universal**	**constant**
what parents say			
public opinion			
the law			
conscience			
what friends say			
family traditions			
a favorite teacher			
horoscope			
what others do			
a pastor			
culture			

2. Do any meet all three criteria for an acceptable standard of truth?

❑ Yes ❑ No

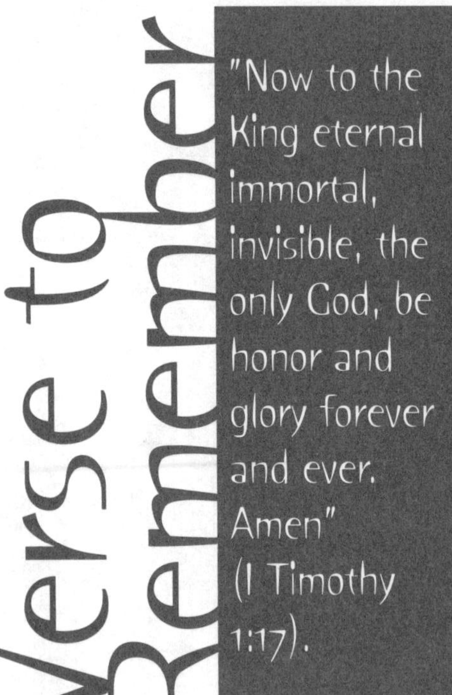

Verse to Remember
"Now to the King eternal immortal, invisible, the only God, be honor and glory forever and ever. Amen"
(I Timothy 1:17).

Understand

Back in the days of Julius Caesar, there was a Roman poet named Horace. Horace criticized the lazy playwrights of his day, who, every time a problem occurred in the plot of a play, brought in one of the many Roman gods to solve it. Horace instructed, "Do not bring a god on to the stage unless the problem is one that deserves a god to solve it (*Right from Wrong* pp.80-81)."

Perhaps you've already discovered that it's impossible to arrive at an objective, universal, and constant standard of truth and morality without bringing God onto the stage. If an objective standard of truth and morality exists, it cannot be the product of the human mind (or it will not be objective); it must be the product of another Mind. If a universal rule of right and wrong exists, it must transcend individual experience (or it will not be universal); it must be above us all, something— or Someone — that is common to all humanity, to all Creation. If a constant and unchanging truth exists, it must reach beyond human timelines (or it would not be constant); it must be eternal.

Those things — those requirements for a standard of truth and morality — are found only in God. He is the source of all truth. He is the standard we need.

Study

1. **He is objective** (fill in the blanks in the verses below to understand God as the objective source of truth):

He is the Rock, his work is _______...a God of _________ and without iniquity, _________ and _________ is he (Deuteronomy 32:4, KJV).

As for God, his way is ___________; the word of the LORD *is __________... For who is God besides the* LORD*? And who is the Rock except our God?* (Psalm 18:30-31).

2. **He is universal** (fill in the blanks in the verses below to understand God as the universal source of truth):

The mountains melt like wax before the Lord, before the Lord ____________ ____________________________ (Psalm 97:5).

The Holy One of Israel is your Redeemer; he is called _______________ ____________________________(Isaiah 54:5).

The Lord has established his throne in heaven, and his kingdom ____________ ____________________________ (Psalm 103:19).

3. **He is constant** (fill in the blanks in the verses below to understand God as the constant source of truth):

Do you not know? Have you not heard? The LORD *is _________________, the Creator of the ends of the earth. He will not grow tired or weary, and his understanding no one can fathom* (Isaiah 40:28).

Everything God does __________________________________; nothing can be added to it and nothing taken from it (Ecclesiastes 3:14).

Apply

• Do you find it easy or difficult to accept God as the only true standard for right and wrong? (chart your response on the line below)

easy ____________________________ difficult

• To what "standard" have you been comparing your behavior up until now?

❑ my own ideas of right and wrong
❑ my parents and what they say
❑ my friends and what they say
❑ my society and what it says
❑ my church and what it says
❑ other ___________________

• Do you think this week's study will affect your actions and attitudes in the future?

❑ Yes ❑ No

If so, in what way?

Pray

Spend a few moments in prayer, responding to today's study; close by praying "Today's Prayer" (above).

Today's Prayer

God of truth, I thank You for what You are teaching me about You, about me, and about truth. When my heart resists Your Word, please soften my heart. When my will rebels against Your teaching, please bend it to Your will. When my mind reflects my ideas, not Yours, please mold it according to Your truth, in Jesus name, Amen.

Chorus/Who makes the rules for me and you/When it's wrong or right is it black and white/Who makes the rules for me and you/It's our life at stake so we better know who makes the rules/

"Who Makes the Rules"
Words and music by
Steven Curtis Chapman,
James Isaac Elliott and
Herb Chapman, Jr.
© 1989 Sparrow Song/New Wings Music

Each of us, whether or not we realize it is faced with a choice between two distinct models of truth, two opposite ways of looking at reality and morality:

Model 1: Truth is defined by God for everyone; it is objective and absolute.
Model 2: Truth is defined by the individual; it is subjective and situational.

The first model acknowledges that God—not man—is central, that God is the source of all things, and that God rules over all. God is the repository of truth, the author and judge of right and wrong.

The second model, on the other hand, places the individual in control of moral matters; because the standard is within the individual, it is particular to that specific person (subjective) and circumstance (situational). In other words, each person considers himself or herself the judge of whatever is right or wrong in any given circumstance. It is an anthropocentric model; that is, it is man-centered, not God-centered. The second model—a relativistic model—is the model most of our culture uses today. It has shaped and molded the way people view the world. It is the lens through which they view life, the basis on which they make life's decisions.

Verse to Remember

"See, I set before you today life and prosperity, death and destruction. For I command you today to love the LORD your God, to walk in his ways, and to keep his commands, decrees and laws" (Deuteronomy 30:15-16).

Read

Carefully and thoughtfully read Deuteronomy 30:11-20, in which Moses spoke to the assembled nation of Israel, and (in effect) recited their choice between adhering to or rejecting God's revelation of truth.

Understand

The land referred to in Moses' speech (vv. 16,18,20) was Canaan, most of which coincides with the modern nation of Israel. God had long ago promised to give this area, though it was populated by several different small nations at this time, to the descendants of Abraham, Isaac, and Jacob (Israel).

Study

1. Moses depicts the choice between adhering to or rejecting God's revelation of truth as a series of contrasts (vv. 15-19). Draw lines to match the following pairs.

life and prosperity	curses
you will live and increase... in the land you are entering	death
blessing	death and destruction
life	you will not live long in the land you are...to enter

2. Which of the two models of truth did Moses command for his people (v. 16)? (circle one)

Model 1: Truth is defined by God for everyone; it is objective and absolute.

Model 2: Truth is defined by the individual; it is subjective and situational.

Today's Prayer

Righteous God, I admit to You my shortcomings and struggles especially ______________________. Please help me to submit to the revelation of Your truth, not only in my beliefs, but in my behavior as well. In the name of Jesus who died and rose again that I might live by His grace, Amen.

3. What do you think Moses meant by saying that the choice between adhering to or rejecting God's revelation of truth was a choice between "life and death, blessings and curses" (v. 19)?

For us, with the rule of right and wrong given us by Christ, there is nothing for which we have no standard.
Tolstoy, War and Peace

reflect

Reflect

• What is the difference between being free to choose to do wrong or right and being free to decide or define what is wrong or right?

• What are the spiritual, physical and emotional consequences of adhering to the second model of truth?

apply

Apply

• Which of the two models of truth do you ascribe to intellectually? Which do you live by?

• Complete the following phrase by circling your choice(s):

"I struggle with. . .
a) knowing what's right
b) doing what's right
c) admitting that God—not me—says what's right
d) none of the above
e) all of the above

pray

Pray

Pray "Today's Prayer" (on this page).

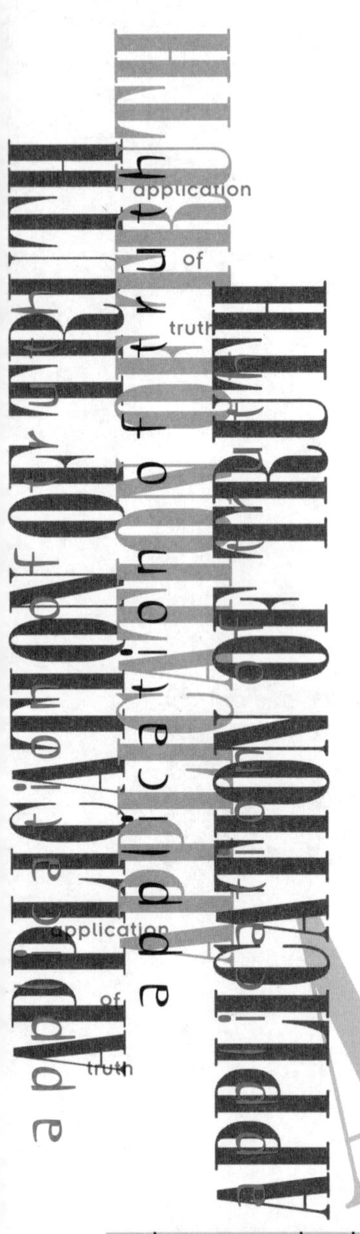

APPLICATION

Get together for food and fellowship with some friends and play the "what if" game of decision making. Each person should have two or three issues needing a decision. Give each person several three by five inch index cards. Have them write an issue on each card. These can be real or imaginary. Choose some issues to write on a poster and discuss what would be the absolute answer and what would be the relative solution. How did you come to this decision?

• Write the words OBJECTIVE, UNIVERSAL, and CONSTANT in bold letters on a three-by-five inch index card. Display the card in a prominent position (mirror, dashboard, etc.) where you will see it several times a day. Each time you see it, quiz yourself about how each of those words applies to morality and truth (for example, "what does the word mean?" and "why must an acceptable standard of truth be objective?").

• It is obvious what some major temptations are for college students: drinking, sex, cheating on tests, or copying a book or disk without getting permission. You could probably add more! Spend 30 minutes by yourself with paper and a pencil and make a list of the not-so-obvious temptations that you face in any given week. Then go back through the list, jotting down what your response to each temptation would be if you accepted the second model of truth. Finally, go through your list once more, noting what your response to each temptation would be if you lived by the first model of truth. Ask God to help you in areas in which you need an extra measure of His grace and mercy.

• Watch television, movies, or real-life situations this week with a discerning eye. Try to discern which model of truth people (real or fictional) use when they face a moral decision. Are they justifying their behavior according to a relativistic model? Are they basing their decisions upon God's revelation of right and wrong? A word of warning: be careful about letting your friends and family know you're watching them!

• The university years are a time many students are "free" for the first time in their lives to do things the way they want to. In the case study, Matthew had taken that freedom and made his lifestyle one of relativism. Make a list of freedoms you have now that you did not have in high school (such as the freedom to make your own schedule, eat what you want, and sleep when you want and for how long!). Would these freedoms change if you had to move back home? If you live at home and commute to school, reflect on the "breaking away" process you went through in becoming a young adult. How did you decide what was appropriate freedom? Were there absolutes involved? Has this list changed since you entered school?

My hope is in what the eye has never seen. Therefore, let me not trust in visible rewards. My hope is in what the heart of man cannot feel. Therefore let me not trust in the feelings of my heart. My hope is what the hand of man has never touched. Do not let me trust what I can grasp between my fingers. Death will loosen my grasp and my vain hope will be gone.
Let my trust be in Your mercy, not in myself. Let my hope be in Your love, not in health, or strength, or ability or human resources.

disciplines for the inner life, by Bob Benson, Sr. and Michael W. Benson, Generoux/Nelson, Nashville, © 1989

APPLICATION

[1] Statistics from the Children's Defense Fund.

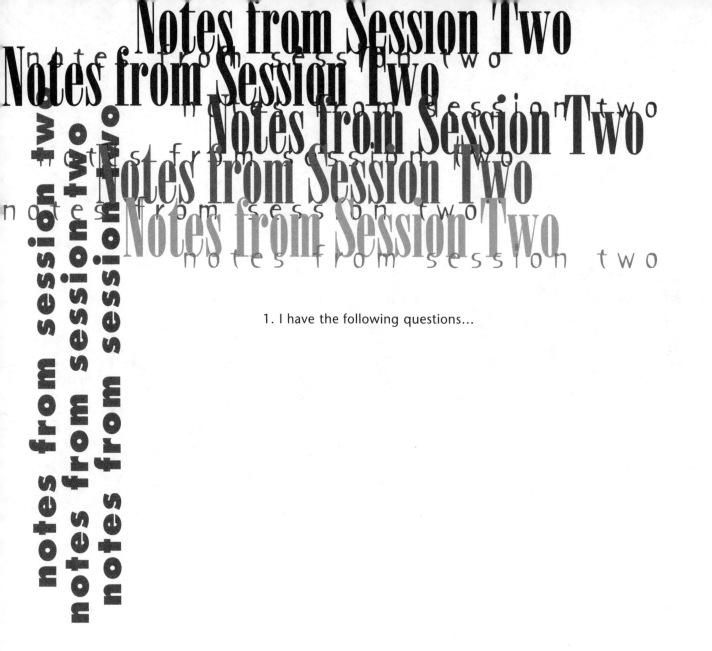

Notes from Session Two

notes from session two
Notes from Session Two
notes from session two
Notes from Session Two
notes from session two
Notes from Session Two
notes from session two
Notes from Session Two
notes from session two
notes from session two
notes from session two
notes from session two

1. I have the following questions...

2. I have the following concerns...

3. Because of this session, I feel...

C. S. Lewis wrote,

> Whenever you find a man who says he does not believe in a real Right and Wrong, you will find the same man going back on this a moment later. He may break his promise to you, but if you try breaking one to him he will be complaining "It's not fair" before you can say Jack Robinson. It seems, then, we are forced to believe in a real Right and Wrong. People may sometimes be mistaken about them, just as people sometimes get their sums wrong; but they are not a matter of mere taste and opinion any more than the multiplication table.[1]

In other words, people may appeal philosophically to the second model of truth (truth is defined by the individual; it is subjective and situational), but they expect others to treat them according to the first model of truth (truth is defined by God for everyone; it is objective and absolute). I have never encountered a single exception to this rule; though I have met people who claimed to be relativists, I have never met a young person who did not expect or demand to be treated fairly. To the old maxim, "There are no atheists in foxholes," I would add a proverb of my own: "There are no relativists in real life."

But for many people, accepting that "a real Right and Wrong" (to use Lewis's wording) exists is not the problem. The question for many people who struggle with questions of right and wrong is, "How do we know a thing is wrong?"

Stephen L. Carter presents the problem this way in his book, *The Culture of Disbelief:*

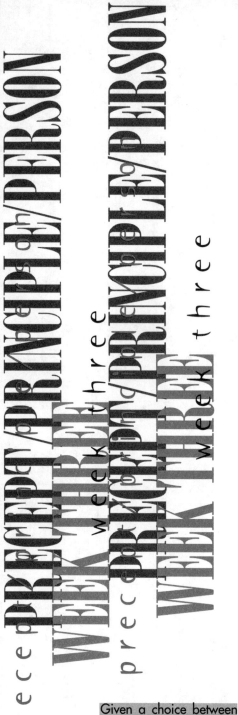

> The hypothesis that dropped objects tend to fall to earth is a hypothesis about the natural world. If one wants to test it according to the rules of natural science, one would...set up an experiment that would yield one result if the hypothesis were false, another if the hypothesis were true — dropping lots of objects, say, and seeing whether they all fall to earth....the trouble with claims about moral knowledge is that even today, more than two centuries after the Enlightenment, we have no settled rules by which to try to determine their truth.[2]

> Given a choice between changing and proving that it is not necessary, most people get busy on the proof.
>
> *—economist John Galbraith*
>
> *"Future Sense: Creating the Future," by H.B. Felatt (The Futurist, September-October 1993)*

The majority of young adults would tend to agree with Stephen Carter. Fifty-six percent (56%) are not convinced that "humans are capable of grasping [moral] knowledge." They tend to believe that "claims about moral knowledge" are simply a matter of opinion.

But that can't be right. If there is any validity at all to "claims about moral knowledge," then there must be a way to discover — and convey — what is right and what is wrong. What we need is, first, to understand that there is an ultimate standard of truth, a standard that exists outside ourselves (or it will not be objective) and above ourselves (or it will not be universal) and beyond our own place and time (or it will not be constant).

But once we are convinced that God is the standard for settling claims about moral knowledge (and that standard, of course, is God), how do we discover — and convey — how that standard applies to specific moral choices?

That need is answered in the test of truth. Webster defines "truth" as "fidelity to an original or standard." As we must do when measuring meters or liters, we must also do in discerning right from wrong; to determine moral truth, we must ask, How does it compare to the original; how does it measure up against the standard?

This week's studies will reveal: a process, a "test," some "settled rules" by which you— or anyone— can discern the truth, and evidence of its benefits.

Newsweek Polls
From what you know about their character, how would you rate the following as role models for young people today? (Percent saying good to excellent role model)
64% Billy Graham
60% Colin Powell
54% Michael Jordan
48% Hillary Clinton
44% Bob Dole
44% Dan Quayle
40% Bill Clinton
38% Ross Perot
25% William Bennett
The Newsweek Poll, June 2-3, 1994

CASE STUDY

Cynthia had no idea that five minutes could last so long! It was only the second week of class, and she had to present a five-minute persuasive speech in her Vocal Communications class. The topic: An influential person in her life.

Several of her classmates had gone before her, and Cynthia was realizing how common was the relativism that Dean Marham preached and Matthew practiced. Of the speeches she had heard, an unusually high number had lauded the influence of people who had urged the speakers to think for themselves, to reject the influence of outside authority in decision-making, to make up their own minds about what was "good and true and right." Many of the influential persons cited in the presentations were faculty or staff members at State. The speeches not only received the approval of Cynthia's professor and fellow students, they began to sound increasingly sensible to Cynthia.

"Ms. Adams, let us hear who has influenced you," the professor said.

Hiding an inner anxiety with a remarkably calm face, Cynthia walked to the front of the class and announced the subject of her speech. "Undoubtedly the most influential person in my life to now has been my mother. Hers has been an influence which, though primarily in our home, church, and community, has been incomparably deep."

She went on to describe her mother, a woman of many abilities who had chosen to raise her children as a full-time vocation. Cynthia described the influence her mother had had on her manners, her personality, her choices, her outlook on life. Her mom's ministry as a Sunday School teacher and example as a committed wife had affected Cynthia in ways in which words could not.

As she began to conclude the speech, she became aware of the cool reception her words were getting. A stony silence presided over her audience, at times pressing toward antagonism.

She faltered over her final sentences, wondering what she had done wrong. Had she violated some unspoken taboo? She found her seat quickly enough and braced for the critique. Several hands shot up before she had even sat down.

Dr. Patterson began the critique innocuously enough. "Ms. Adams, you organize your thoughts very well. I found your speech well-conceived and direct. Does the class have any comments on the structure of Ms. Adams' speech?"

The hands went down.

He then continued, "How about the direction of her persuasion? How effective was Ms. Adams in convincing you of her mother's influence?"

The hands returned.

"Ms. Jacoby."

"I found the speech more pitiable than persuasive. It seems like this

CASE STUDY

woman has reconciled herself to being a victim of the sexist oppression that women have fought for years. Rather than wasting her talents and time being a maid and cook to her family, I would have been more impressed and influenced by her getting a degree and making a difference in society."

Another hand.

"Yeah, what's so influential about being a housewife? Why would someone let herself be manipulated into spending her entire life like that? Women have so many opportunities to really influence the world, even by volunteering with an environmental group or a social justice organization."

Though several others spoke, Cynthia couldn't listen to any more of the criticisms. She wasn't sure whether to argue or cry — or both. She had always admired her mother, but now — for the first time in her life — she was beginning to feel embarrassed. . . not only for her mom, but for herself.

She began to wonder, Have I been too sheltered all these years? She remembered Matthew's words: "My parents would tell me one thing, my teachers and friends another, and the preacher still something else. . .When I got here to State, I finally started to think for myself." Maybe that's my problem, she thought. Maybe it's time for me to think for myself, too.

"These kids today. They're soft. They don't know how good they have it. Not only did they never have to fight in a war...they never even had to dodge one."
New Republic columnist Michael Kinsley

"generalizations x" by Jeff Giles (Newsweek, 6/6/94)

Questions

1. How do you respond to Cynthia's experience?

2. Why do you think the class criticized the speech?

3. What is inconsistent about their criticism?

If, as we have seen, there exists an absolute standard of truth, then it must be God for only He possesses the necessary qualifications. And if God is the standard, then it would be reasonable to expect God to have revealed the standard to us. And, indeed, we find that is precisely the case.

As Moses told the people of Israel, God's revelation of truth "is not too difficult for you or beyond your reach. It is not up in heaven, so that you have to ask, 'Who will ascend into heaven to get it and proclaim it to us so we may obey it?' Nor is it beyond the sea, so that you have to ask, 'Who will cross the sea to get it and proclaim it to us so we may obey it?' No, the word is very near you; it is in your mouth and in your heart so you may obey it" (Deuteronomy 30:11-14).

Exodus 3:1-22

Now Moses was tending the flock of Jethro his father-in-law, the priest of Midian, and he led the flock to the far side of the desert and came to Horeb, the mountain of God. There the angel of the LORD appeared to him in flames of fire from within a bush. Moses saw that though the bush was on fire it did not burn up. So Moses thought, "I will go over and see this strange sight— why the bush does not burn up."

When the LORD saw that he had gone over to look, God called to him from within the bush, "Moses! Moses!"

And Moses said, "Here I am."

"Do not come any closer," God said."Take off your sandals, for the place where you are standing is holy ground." Then he said, "I am the God of your father, the God of Abraham, the God of Isaac and the God of Jacob." At this, Moses hid his face, because he was afraid to look at God.

The LORD said, "I have indeed seen the misery of my people in Egypt. I have heard them crying out because of their slave drivers, and I am concerned about their suffering. So I have come down to rescue them from the hand of the Egyptians and to bring them up out of that land into a good and spacious land, a land flowing with milk and honey—the home of the Canaanites, Hittites, Amorites, Perizzites, Hivites and Jebusites. And now the cry of the Israelites has reached me, and I have seen the way the Egyptians are oppressing them. So now, go. I am sending you to Pharaoh to bring my people the Israelites out of Egypt."

But Moses said to God, "Who am I, that I should go to Pharaoh and bring the Israelites out of Egypt?"

And God said, "I will be with you. And this will be the sign to you that it is I who have sent you: When you have brought the people out of Egypt, you will worship God on this mountain."

Moses said to God, "Suppose I go to the Israelites and say to them, `The God of your fathers has sent me to you,' and they ask me, `What is his name?' Then what shall I tell them?"

God said to Moses, "I AM WHO I AM. This is what you are to say to the Israelites: `I AM has sent me to you.'"

God also said to Moses, "Say to the Israelites, `The LORD, the God of your fathers—the God of Abraham, the God of Isaac and the God of Jacob—has sent me to you.' This is my name for ever, the name by which I am to be remembered from generation to generation.

"Go, assemble the elders of Israel and say to them, `The LORD, the God of your fathers—the God of Abraham, Isaac and Jacob—appeared to me and said: I have watched over you and have seen what has been done to you in Egypt. And I have promised to bring you up out of your misery in Egypt into the land of the Canaanites, Hittites, Amorites, Perizzites, Hivites and Jebusites—a land flowing with milk and honey.'

"The elders of Israel will listen to you. Then you and the elders are to go to the king of Egypt and say to him, `The LORD, the God of the Hebrews, has met with us. Let us take a three-day journey into the desert to offer sacrifices to the LORD our God.' But I know that the king of Egypt will not let you go unless a mighty hand compels him. So I will stretch out my hand and strike the Egyptians with all the wonders that I will perform among them. After that, he will let you go.

"And I will make the Egyptians favourably disposed towards this people, so that when you leave you will not go empty-handed. Every woman is to ask her neighbour and any woman living in her house for articles of silver and gold and for clothing, which you will put on your sons and daughters. And so you will plunder the Egyptians."

Read
As a group, carefully read Exodus 3:1-22.

Discuss
1. God not only revealed Himself to Moses in the desert, He revealed Himself in several ways. How did God attract Moses' attention? Why do you think He chose that particular method? Discuss.

2. How did God reveal Himself in verse 6? Why do you think He revealed Himself in that way? Discuss.

3. How did God reveal Himself in verses 7-8?

- As a God who_______________("I have indeed seen the misery of my people")
- As a God who_________________ ("I have heard them crying out")
- As a God who__________________("I am concerned about their suffering")
- As a God who_____________________("So I have come down to rescue them")

4. How did God reveal Himself in answer to Moses' question in verse 13? Why do you think Moses had to ask God's name? What name(s) did God give in response? Discuss.

5. For what purpose did God reveal Himself (vv. 16-22). Does that relate to this study? If so, how? Discuss.

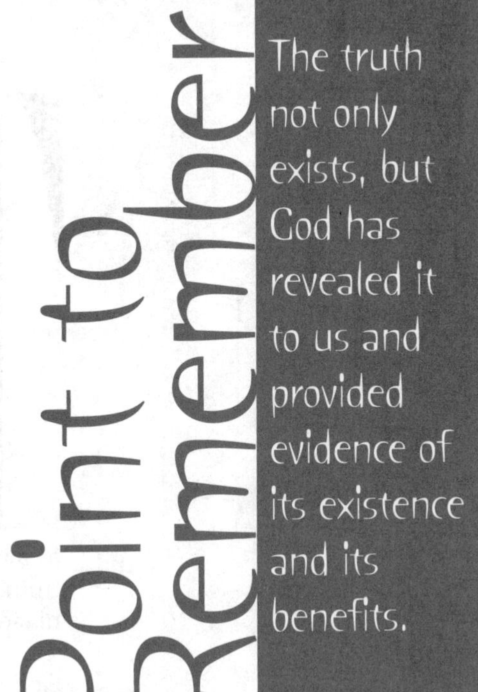

Point to Remember
The truth not only exists, but God has revealed it to us and provided evidence of its existence and its benefits.

Today's Prayer

Father God, we acknowledge You as a righteous God, the standard of all that is right and good. Help us to learn Your Word, to discern Your truth, and to turn from our willful ways, through the love and light of Your Holy Spirit. Amen.

For many Christian Xers, the issue is not the evils of pop culture but how stagnant the arts seem to be within the evangelical church. To the buster crowd, Christian music often feels old-fashioned or, if contemporary, not up to the highest standards. There also seems to be a yearning for art that is not didactic...

"Reaching the First Post-Christian Generation," by Andres Tapia (Christianity Today, September 12, 1994)

Reflect
1. What is the significance of the realization that God is a God who reveals Himself? How does it relate to our study of the moral maze?

For Further Discussion
1. God revealed Himself to Moses in a burning bush, and apparently in an audible voice; how do you think He reveals Himself (and His truth) to us today?

2. Does God's revelation mean we don't have to think for ourselves? What do you think Moses might say to Cynthia about her desire to think for herself?

Pray
Review the divine attributes God revealed to Moses (see question 3 above) and spend a few moments in prayer, praising God for those attributes, and for how He reveals them in your life.

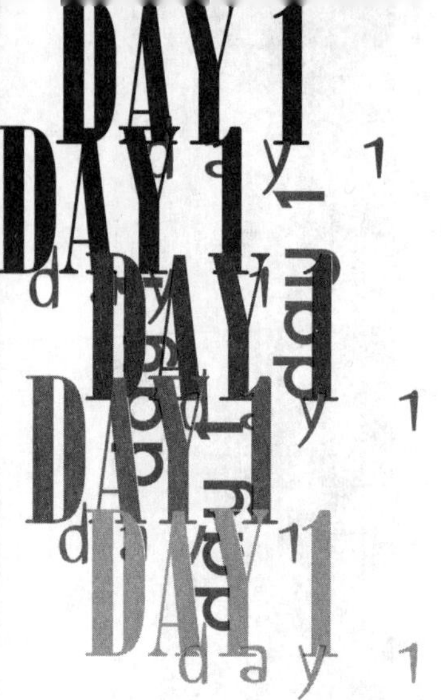

The very first recorded words of God to man appear in the Eden account:

You are free to eat of any tree in the garden; but you must not eat from the tree of the knowledge of good and evil, for when you eat of it you will surely die (Genesis 2:16-17).

The man and woman in the garden already possessed the knowledge of good. They were surrounded by every imaginable blessing: a lush garden watered by a sparkling river and populated with birds and beasts, fruit trees and flowering shrubs. But God's first recorded words to man marked a moral choice, a choice between good and evil. With His first command to humanity, God identified Himself as a moral being, the definer of right and wrong, the source of absolute truth. God drew a line around that tree, a line that clearly marked the difference between right and wrong.

God spoke to Eve after she and her husband had eaten of the forbidden fruit. God inquired, "What is this you have done?" You see, God was revealing Himself to the man and woman as the arbiter of good and evil, as the righteous Judge, who would punish them by cursing them and expelling them from the garden.

Point to Remember

Like a parent teaching a young child, the most elementary means by which the God of truth revealed Himself to men and women was by precept.

When God spoke to Cain, who had murdered his brother Abel, He asked, "What have you done?" God revealed Himself as the God of life, who abhors murder. He cursed Cain and banished him to the land of Nod.

Throughout the pages of Scripture, God reveals Himself as the source of absolute truth. He disclosed Himself to Noah as a righteous God who rewards righteousness and punishes wickedness. He proved Himself to Abraham as a trustworthy God who keeps promises. He showed Himself to David as a God of mercy. And through Jesus Christ, He proved supremely that He was a God of transcending love.

The revelation of God — in the Bible, in the Incarnation, and sometimes even through His body, the Church — reveals Himself as the fountain of truth, the origin of morality. Today's study focuses on the primary, most elementary way in which God makes Himself known to us, even today. It is the first of a three-part "Test of Truth."

Think Thru

1. Check the following statements you remember your parents saying?

- ❑ "Don't play with matches."
- ❑ "Don't touch a hot stove."
- ❑ "Say please and thank you."
- ❑ "Don't run with scissors!"
- ❑ "Don't sit so close to the T.V."
- ❑ "Mind your manners."
- ❑ "Look both ways before you cross the street."

Each of those phrases is a precept. When you were a child, the communication between you and your parents was mostly in the form of precept. They repeatedly told you "do this," and "don't do that."

Similarly, God has issued precepts — we usually call them commands — to His people. He has told us, "do this," and "don't do that," in language as clear as your parents telling you to "look both ways before you cross the street."

Study

Look up the verses below in your Bible and complete each precept:

1. "You shall ______________________________" (Ex. 20:3).
2. "Do not ______________________________" (Matt. 7:1).
3. "Do not ______. Do not ______. Do not __________" (Lev. 19:11).
4. "Avoid ______________________________" (I Thess. 4:3).
5. "You shall not ______________"(Deut. 5:17).
6. "Love ____________________" (John 13:34).
7. "Obey ____________________ and ______________________

______________________" (Hebrews 13:17).

Understand

The precepts above are just a few of the commands God gives in His word (Jewish tradition maintains that God gave over 600 specific commands!).

Reflect

God has communicated a lot about Himself to us through precept. God's commands reveal what He likes, what He doesn't like, what He considers important, what He thinks is good, and what He thinks is bad. But few people realize that precept — the rules, regulations, codes, and requirements of Scripture —is but the first step in understanding basic morality. The precepts of the Lord are not just a bunch of do's and don'ts, shalts and shalt-nots; they are designed also to lead us beyond the precept to the next step in the process of truth.

Apply

Complete the following sentences aloud to express your response to today's study.

I'm feeling...
I'm thinking...
I'm having trouble...
I'm starting to realize...
God's speaking to me through His Word. He's saying...

Pray

Take a few moments to respond in prayer to what God's word is teaching you.

Today's Prayer

God of truth, I praise You and thank You because You love me. Remind me that Your precepts, Your commands, are one of the ways You have expressed Your love. Help me to obey You, as a loving child, in Jesus' name, Amen.

If all of God's commands are the first step toward discerning right from wrong, principles are the next step on the stairway, because behind each precept is a principle.

A principle is a rule or standard that may be applied to more than one type of situation. For example, your mom's precept to "say please and thank you" at the dinner table only applied to mealtimes. Your sociology professor's dumb rule about addressing all your fellows students as "Mr." and "Ms." applies only to his class. The prohibition against loud music in the dorm takes effect after midnight. All these different precepts apply to specific situations, but the comprehensive principle behind each specific precept is courtesy or respect. The precept is specific; the principle is general.

Principles help explain the "why" behind a command. A concern for safety is one of the principles behind a mother's command to look both ways before crossing the street. Reverence for life is the principle behind the command, "Thou shalt not kill." A principle behind the command, "You shall not give false testimony," is honesty.

Learning to identify the principles behind God's precepts will help us see the overarching truth that applies, even when a specific command doesn't seem to apply.

Read

Carefully and thoughtfully read Exodus 20:1-17. As you read, try to identify the principle behind each precept (for example, the principle behind the first commandment in verse 3, is the sovereignty of God).

Understand

Jewish tradition numbers the "Ten Commandments" differently than Christian tradition; in Jewish reckoning, verse 2 is the first commandment (which Christian readers generally view as preliminary to the commandments, also called the "decalogue," literally "ten words").

Study

Look up the following verses in your Bible and draw a line to match the precepts with the principles they express on the right.

Precept	**Principle**
Exodus 20:15	Purity
Exodus 23:9	Respect
Matthew 5:42	Honesty
Ephesians 6:1	Mercy
1 John 3:11	Self-Control
Isaiah 58:7	Unity
Ephesians 5:4	Justice
1 Corinthians 6:18	Love
Genesis 2:24	Generosity

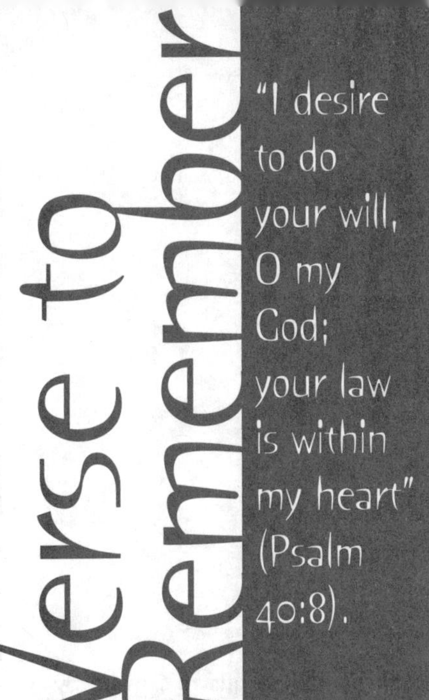

Reflect

• Do you think it's important to identify the principles behind God's precepts? Why or why not?

• How might an understanding of the principles behind God's commands help you to make right choices in circumstances where there a specific command doesn't seem to apply?

• If, as Jewish tradition maintains, God gave over 600 distinct commands, will there be as many principles expressed in those precepts? More? Fewer?

Apply

• Have you disobeyed any of the above precepts today? This week? If so, what?

• Has your life displayed any of the above principles today? This week? If so, what?

• Do you react differently to the precepts than you do to the principles? If so, in what way? If so, why do you think that is?

Today's Prayer

Father, I seek to have Your law in my heart. Beyond the laws, though, help me to see the righteous principles behind Your commands, that I might understand them—and You—better. But even when I don't understand, help me to do Your will, and obey Your law, in the name of Jesus, who alone can enable me to do that. Amen.

Pray

What do you wish to say to God in response to today's study? Write your response below.

Knowing God's precepts, and even the principles of truth that lie behind those precepts, is not the end of the story. The process of discerning truth — of distinguishing right from wrong — leads from precept, through principle, to the Person of God Himself. That's "the rest of the story."

Too many people focus on God's law, and never see its extensions — what it teaches us about the character of God. You see, ultimately, the reason we have this concept that some things are right and some things are wrong is because there exists a Creator, Jehovah God, and He is a righteous God. The reason we think that there are such things as "fair" and "unfair" is because our Maker is a just God. The reason love is a virtue and hatred a vice is because the God who formed us is a God of love. The reason honesty is right and deceit is wrong is because God is true. The reason chastity is moral and promiscuity is immoral is because God is pure. The ultimate purpose of God in every precept is to bring us to the knowledge of Himself, because He desires a relationship with us. We can only know truth by knowing the God of truth.

> Man needs the answers given by God in the Bible to have adequate answers not only for how to be in an open relationship with God, but also for how to know the present meaning of life and how to have final answers in distinguishing right and wrong.
>
> *Francis Schaeffer, How Should We Then Live?, pg. 81*

Read

Look up Exodus 33:13, Moses' request to God after receiving the Law. Write the verse on the lines below:

____

____

____

____

read

Verse to Remember

"The law of the LORD is perfect, reviving the soul. The statutes of the LORD are trustworthy, making wise the simple. The precepts of the LORD are right, giving joy to the heart. The commands of the LORD are radiant, giving light to the eyes. The fear of the LORD is pure, enduring forever. The ordinances of the LORD are sure and altogether righteous" (Psalm 19:7-9).

Study

1. Moses' words reveal that he had two goals. What were they?

1) ________________________________

2) ________________________________

study

2. What did he want God to do to help him achieve those goals? (Check all that apply)

- ❑ pay his college tuition
- ❑ give him super-human powers
- ❑ teach him God's ways
- ❑ make him popular

3. What do you think Moses means when he says, "teach me your ways?"

4. How could learning God's ways help Moses to know God and find favor with Him?

Reflect

• God's law is not an end in itself. Some of His commands were illustrative, others were practical, but all were — and are — an expression of His character.

• The truth resides in the commands of God because those commands were given by the God of truth. The truth would not cease being true if the Law were to disappear from the face of the earth, nor would it cease to be true if there were no humans to discern the principle — because the truth resides in the person of God Himself, who is eternal. We can more effectively determine right from wrong when we look to God — His nature and character — as the measure of truth and morality.

> As with reading or eating, much depends on what you're taking in — or taken in by...Engagement with Scripture and the great doctrines of the Christian faith is the greatest source of health for Christians. Nothing makes sick theology and morality healthier than being exposed to healthy theology and morality. Spirituality thrives on right belief.
>
> *"Testing the Spiritualities," by James R. Edwards (Christianity Today, September 12, 1994)*

Today's Prayer

Giver of the Law, I praise You because You are perfect, You are trustworthy, You are right, You are radiant, You are pure, You are sure, and altogether righteous, like the commands You have given. Teach me Your ways, so that I may know You, in the name of Your Son, Jesus, Amen.

Apply

• How could learning God's ways help you distinguish and defend right from wrong?

• How could you apply yourself today to "learning God's ways?"

Pray

Prayerfully read Psalm 19:7-9, and close with "Today's Prayer" (on this page), thanking God for His attributes (perfect, sure, right, radiant, pure, and righteous) which are revealed in His law.

The test of truth determines the rightness or wrongness of an action or attitude by tracing a specific precept through the principle and to the very person and character of God Himself. Making a habit of such an approach to moral decisions will solve many problems and answer many questions. But the way out of the moral maze involves, not only the test of truth, but the evidence of truth as well.

You see, a lot of people — Christians included — see God's commands as constricting. They think that biblical morality is confining. But God's commands, like those of a loving parent — "don't touch the stove," "look both ways before you cross the street," "eat your vegetables" — are not meant to spoil our fun and make us miserable.

Each divorce is the death of a small civilization.
Pat Conroy in "An Outlaw Mom Tells All" (Ms., Jan/Feb 1995)

On the contrary, God gave commands, such as "Flee sexual immorality," and "Husbands, love your wives," and "You shall not steal," and all other commands because there are immeasurable benefits to a moral lifestyle. God didn't throw those precepts into the Bible just because He liked the way they sounded; God didn't concoct those rules to be a killjoy or to throw His weight around; God gave those commands because He knew some things we didn't. He knew (and still knows) the surest path to pleasure and fulfillment, as well as the way to emptiness and frustration; his precepts -because they are a reflection of His nature and character— will lead us into the former and away from the latter.

Read

Reread Exodus 20:1-17.

Understand

The third commandment (against misusing the name of God) was originally understood as referring primarily to swearing a false oath; later, however, God's people came to regard it as a prohibition against any light or thoughtless use of the divine name (so much so, in fact, that it became forbidden to speak the name "Yahweh," as a means of preventing its misuse).

Study

1. God issued His commands to protect us. Complete the table below by filling in possible ways that each of the commandments might protect those who obey them.

COMMANDMENT	PROTECTION
I You shall have no other gods before me	
II You shall not make for yourself an idol. You shall not bow down to them or worship them	
III You shall not misuse the name of the LORD your God	
IV Remember the Sabbath day (day of rest) by keeping it holy	

V Honour your father and your mother

VI You shall not murder

VI You shall not commit adultery

VIII You shall not steal

IX You shall not give false testimony against your neighbour

X You shall not covet

Reflect

• Since God's motivation in giving His commands to us is one of love and protection, the first commandment ("You shall have no other gods before me") functions like a parent who warns a young child not to go anywhere with strangers; it warns us listen to the One who has pledged Himself to protect us, not harm us.

• Should we obey God's commands because they're good for us. . . or because they're right?

• Do God's precepts accomplish other things (besides protecting us)? If so, what?

Apply

• How do you respond to today's study? How does it make you feel? What does it make you think?

• The protection afforded by obedience to God's commands is not a one-time event; it is daily. What problems, frustrations, or troubles have you avoided today as a result of obeying God?

• What problems, frustrations, or troubles have you avoided in the past as a result of obeying God?

• Have you thanked God for His protection?

Today's Prayer

Loving Father, thank You for the protection Your commands provide. Remind me, today and every day, that Your commandments and statutes are for my good, and help me, through the presence of Your Holy Spirit, to follow Your ways, not my own, in Jesus' name, Amen.

Pray

Pray "Today's Prayer" (on this page).

Verse to Remember

"And now, Israel, what does the LORD your God require from you, but to fear the LORD your God, to walk in all His ways and love Him, and to serve the LORD your God with all your heart and with all your soul, and to keep the LORD's commandments and His statutes which I am commanding you today for your good?" (Deuteronomy 10:12-13, NASB).

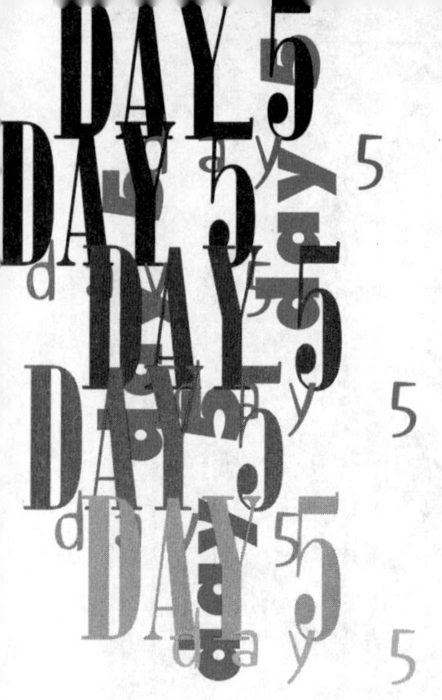

God's loving motivation to protect us from harm and frustration is only half of the evidence of truth. The evidence of truth also supports the conclusion that God's precepts provide for us.

The Right From Wrong study of churched young adults illustrates the clear benefits of a moral lifestyle. The young adults who were most discontented with their lives, by their own admission, were those who had already had sexual intercourse, those from broken homes, and those who rejected the existence of absolute truth and objective standards of morality.

In other words, the results of the study strongly suggest that immoral behavior produces negative results. It indicates that moral behavior makes young adults more likely to say they are satisfied with their lives, that they have high hopes, that they are respected by others. The study intimates that morality breeds a healthy self-esteem, making a person more likely to characterize himself or herself as "an achiever," "encouraged," and "reliable."

Immoral behavior, on the other hand, fosters negative attitudes, making a person more likely to say that he or she is "resentful," "lonely," "angry with life," "unmotivated," "disappointed," "confused," "skeptical," mistrustful of others, and lacking in purpose. (*Right from Wrong,* p.259)

Read

Carefully and thoughtfully read Jeremiah 29:11.

read

Understand

The words of this passage were written to the people of God who were living in exile in Babylon, many miles from their home. They had suffered many calamities as a result of their disregard of God's commands. Though these words were written thousands of years ago to a specific group of people, they illustrate God's loving motivation of protecting and providing for us today.

understand

Verse to Remember:

"For I know the plans I have for you," declares the LORD, "plans to prosper you and not to harm you, plans to give you hope and a future" (Jeremiah 29:11).

Study

Answer the following questions based on Jeremiah 29:11.

1. According to this verse, who knows the plans God has for you? (circle one)
   - a. The Shadow
   - b. Your professors
   - c. Only you
   - d. Your parents
   - e. God

2. What kind of plans are they?

3. Does this verse refer to God's protection and provision? How?

study

4. Next, turn another page or two in your Bible to Jeremiah 32:39-41, in which God talks about what He desires for those who follow Him. Why does God want people to fear Him and obey Him?

5. What does God rejoice in?

6. Imagine God's protection and provision as the two sides of a coin. If you were the engraver, how would you design a coin illustrating the evidence of truth?

sample

Today's Prayer

Caring Father, thank You for Your loving motivation to protect me and provide for me. Remind me every day that Your precepts are for my good, and help me to submit to them, and to Your plans for me, in the name of Jesus, who always did Your will, Amen.

Reflect

• Do the above verses make it sound like God wants to spoil your fun or prevent you from enjoying the best life has to offer?

• Think back on yesterday's study of the Ten Commandments and the protection they afford. In what ways does obedience to those commands not only protect you from negative things but also provide positive things for you?

• Do you think the fact that God's precepts are for our good make them right? In other words, is the truth right because it works?

• Does the evidence of truth guarantee that people who do right will never suffer?

"I want to be different from other girls. I want a guy to look at me in another way. I want to have respect for myself. I see girls getting into trouble, and I don't want to get hurt. I want to be a virgin."

—Betsy, teenager
"Virgin Cool," by Michele Ingrassia (Newsweek 10/17/94)

Apply

• How do you find yourself responding to today's study? How does it make you feel? What does it make you think?

• Like God's protection, the provision afforded by obedience to God's commands is not a one-time event; it is daily. Are there any ways that God has provided blessing, peace, or strength as a result of obeying God?

• Have you thanked God for His provision?

Pray

Using Jeremiah 29:11 as a guide, spend a few moments in prayer, thanking God for the plans He has for you, and submitting to His perfect will.

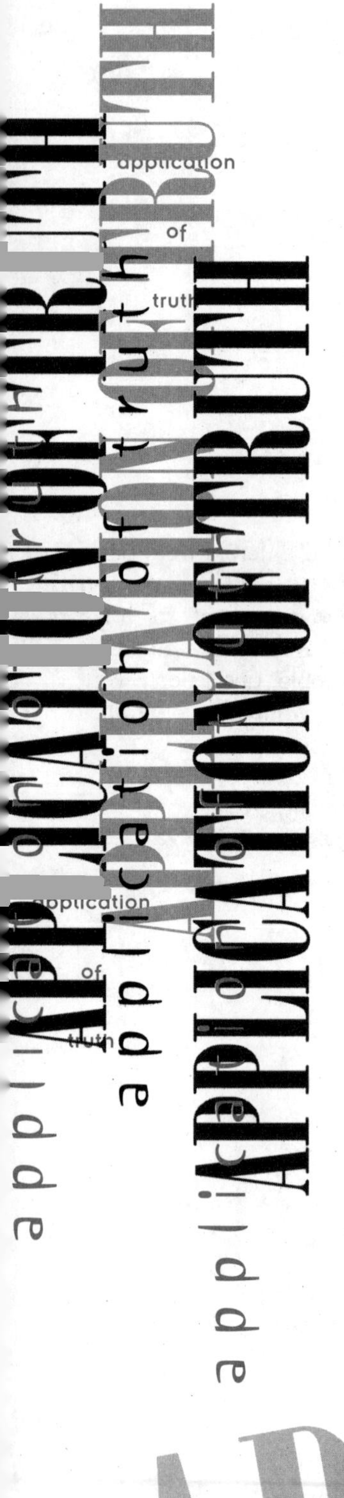

Remember Cynthia's address on the most influential person in her life? Conduct a similar exercise, writing a page or two of reflection on the most influential person in your life. Why do you admire him or her? What qualities does he or she possess that you would like to develop yourself? Do you think your most influential person believes in an absolute standard of truth? Does his or her behavior reflect that belief?

• Use everyday routines to reinforce your understanding of the test of truth. Trace moral decision decisions — even those you normally don't think about — through the precept-principle-person process. For example, why is it right to return an item you borrowed from your roommate? Other opportunities to review the test of truth may be suggested by the following situations:

the lyrics of a popular song on the radio

studying for a test

paying for a purchase at the mall

waiting your turn in traffic

keeping a date with a friend

referees' calls and penalties at a sporting event

• C. S. Lewis said, "Virtue — even attempted virtue — brings light; indulgence brings fog" (from *Mere Christianity*). Copy that quote on a three-by-five inch card and tape it on your bathroom mirror. The next time your mirror fogs up, reflect on Lewis's words and remind yourself of the protection and provision that result from following God's commands.

• Construct a cardboard model of the coin you drew on page 67. Carry it in your pocket or purse to remind you of the protection and provision of God's commands.

APPLICATION

• Picture the test of truth as three lenses through which you can discern truth:

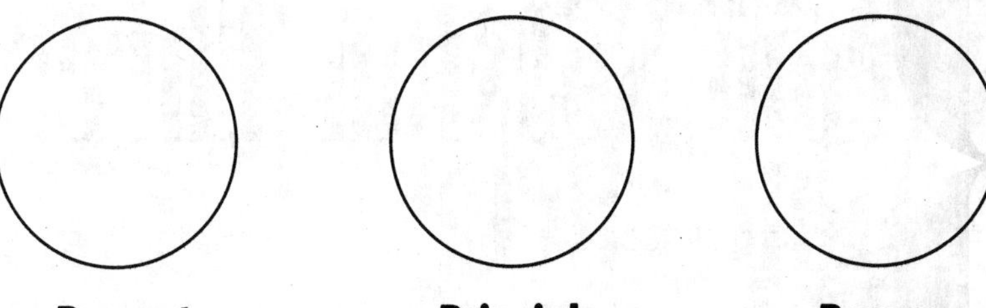

Precept **Principle** **Person**

APPLICATION

If you wear glasses or contact lenses, use the occasion of putting your lenses on (or in) to review the precept-principle-person process for discerning absolute truth.

[1] C.S. Lewis, *Mere Christianity*, (New York: Macmillan Publishing Co.,1943).

[2] Stephen L. Carter, *The Culture of Disbelief* (New York: BasicBooks, 1993).

Notes from Session Three

1. I have the following questions...

2. I have the following concerns...

3. Because of this session, I feel...

...in the supersexed world of pop culture, the image of abstinence is shifting from the pimply dweeb who can't get a date; virgin geek is giving way to virgin chic. Winsome rocker Juliana Hatfield, 26, announced her virginity a few years back, in Interview magazine, no less. MTV veejay Kennedy declared her virginity with a whatcha'-gonna-make-of-it air. NBA star A. C. Green has his own athletes-for-abstinence campaign. And up and down the TV channels, writers who once rushed characters into bed are hot to keep them out. Witness virgin goddess Tori Spelling, whose "Beverly Hills 90210" character clings to her virtue even when she feels like the last virgin on Rodeo Drive. And though the fictional Sarah Owens gave up her chastity on "Models, Inc.," Cassidy Rae, the 18-year-old actress who plays her, has become virginity's most visible standard-bearer. "I want to stay as pure as I can for my [future] husband," Cassidy says.

"Virgin Cool," by Michele Ingrassia (Newsweek 10/17/94)

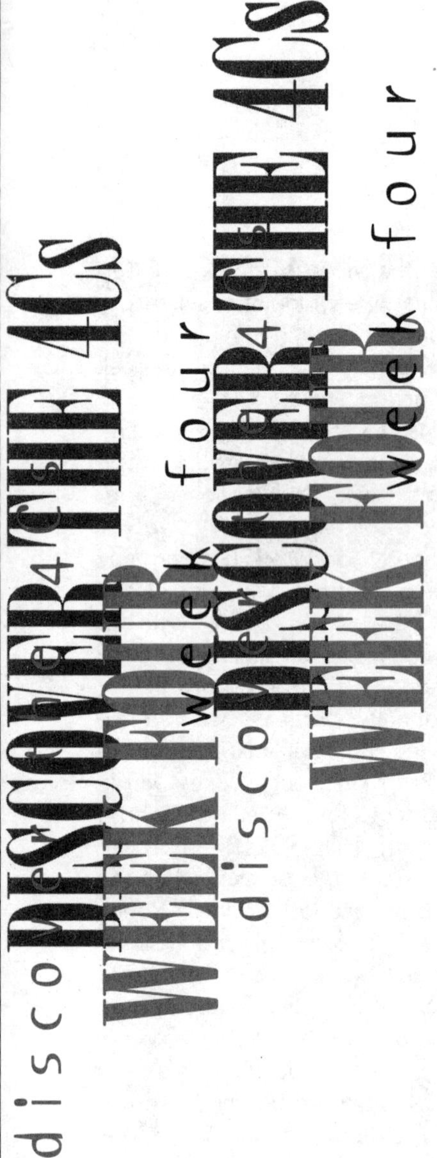

At first all you see is a repetitive design of colors and shapes. But if you hold the design close to your face and slowly move it farther away without refocusing your eyes, you begin to see another image, a multi-dimensional form where before there was only a flat picture.

That's the key to discerning the hidden "5-D" images that decorate millions of posters, books, and postcards. Some people say that they just can't seem to unlock the secret; others can glance at a "5-D" design and almost instantly discern the image. It seems simple to the people in the latter group; once you get the knack of focusing your eyes beyond the surface image, you can see clearly.

That experience has its parallel in matters of ethics and morality. Once you change the way you look at the confusion, it suddenly makes sense. When you are equipped with the proper truth view, you will be better able to identify what truths are absolute and what makes them absolute... and you will have a chance to make the right choices. Once you acknowledge that the distinction between right and wrong is objective (it is defined outside ourselves—it is not subjectively determined), universal (it is for all people in all places; it does not change from person to person or place to place), and constant (it is for all times—it does not change from day to day), you adopt a moral and ethical viewpoint that guides your perception of what is right and what is wrong. Your "truth view" acts as a lens through which you see all of life and its many choices.

Yet that is not the end of the battle, because many people still choose to do wrong, even when they know it's wrong. Many people still choose wrong, even when they know their choice may have devastating consequences. Why? Because wrong choices very often offer immediate benefits, while right choices seem to offer more long-range benefits. Sin is usually packaged very appealingly, and it carries a promise of immediate satisfaction. That is why so many choose sin; it offers instant gratification. Right choices, on the other hand, often require postponing satisfaction for better long-term benefits.

> People have presuppositions, and they will live more consistently on the basis of these presuppositions than even they themselves may realize. By presuppositions we mean the basic way an individual looks at life, his basic world view, the grid through which he sees the world.
>
> *Francis Schaeffer, How Should We Then Live?, pg. 19*

A young woman from a Christian family started dating a guy on the football team. She was a pretty young woman, but she had never been very popular with boys. Early in her relationship with the football player, she had sex with him. Soon afterward, they broke up, but her former boyfriend encouraged a teammate to go out with her. She went from that football player to another. Before long, she had slept with the whole football team.

By the time her parents learned of their daughter's behavior, it had been going on for months. They sat down with their daughter and told her they knew what had been going on and cried with her. Then they asked her, "Why did you do this?" The only explanation she offered was,"I just wanted to feel loved. It never lasted for very long, and I always felt bad about it afterward, but at least for a few fleeting moments I felt like someone loved me."

You see, she had accepted a counterfeit. She had been suckered by the appealing short-term benefits of the wrong choice. But people don't want a few fleeting moments or the lonely thrills they get from a false love. They want the real thing. Without solid convictions about truth, however, people will buy the counterfeits almost every time. It's a downward spiral. When they reject truth as an objective standard, their view of life becomes distorted. When their view becomes distorted, they easily accept the counterfeits. When they accept the counterfeits, they begin to make wrong choices. When they make wrong choices, they suffer the consequences. The choice is, quite literally, truth or consequences.

There is a way, however, to counter the craving for instant gratification. There is a way to recognize the counterfeits. There is a way to choose right even when wrong is packaged appealingly. There is a process by which you can not only discern what is right, but do it. That's what this week's studies are all about.

CASE STUDY

Cynthia bent over her Intro to Psychology text, struggling to focus her thoughts; it wasn't easy with the raucous sounds of another Friday night on her floor. Her roommate, Teri, breezed into the room.

"Hi, Teri," Cynthia offered.

Teri threw a nod and a grunted greeting across the room. She tossed her backpack onto her bed and peered at her reflection in the mirror.

She turned to Cynthia a moment later, after licking her fingers and smoothing her full eyebrows. "Hey," she said, "why don't you take a break and come with me for a change? You gotta get your nose outta those books once in a while, you know?"

Cynthia smiled. She and Teri got along pretty well, but they'd never done anything together. Teri ran with a totally different crowd from Cynthia; *actually,* Cynthia admitted to herself, I don't have a crowd.

She had been at State for almost two months, and hadn't really fit in with any of the people in her dorm. Several students, like Matthew and Rosemarie, her orientation leaders, had been friendly enough, but they were all so...well, so *different* from her. They liked to argue about social issues, or go out drinking, or party for most of the weekend. She did occasionally see Jesse, the guy from her high school, but he was a computer major, and they just didn't have much in common.

"Whaddya say?" Teri asked without looking at Cynthia. She touched up her thick lipstick in the mirror.

Cynthia shrugged. "Where are you going?"

"A bunch of us are going to 'Skeeters.' They're serving orange beer all weekend...you know, for Halloween. Everybody's going to be there."

Cynthia hesitated. The orange beer didn't appeal to her, but she figured she needed to start making friends sometime. She wasn't helping herself by staying in her room. Teri's offer was very tempting. She suddenly lifted a hand to her hair. *I can't go out looking like this.* She glanced at her sweatshirt-and-sweatpants ensemble. *I'm a mess!*

"Not this time, Teri," she said. "I mean, look at me. I look awful!"

Teri flashed a glance at Cynthia's rumpled form and shrugged. She didn't argue with her roommate's assessment of her appearance. "Well, if you change your mind, you know where to find me." She waved and ducked through the door.

Cynthia watched the door close and kicked herself. *That does it,* she told herself. *I'm not my mommy's little girl anymore. The next time Teri invites me out for a little fun, I'm going to take her up on her offer. Why should she have all the fun?*

She studied a while longer, then listened to music for about an hour before going to sleep...early...on a Friday night. Hours later, she was awakened by someone pounding on her door. She opened it to see a slumped Teri hanging between Rosemarie and some guy Cynthia did not know.

"She's wasted," the guy said.

Cynthia swung the door wide and switched the ceiling light on. The flash of brightness roused Teri, whose head rose. Her eyes opened without focusing and she raised a hand to her mouth, but too late — she began to vomit all over herself and her two caretakers. Cynthia and Rosemarie undressed Teri and dropped her onto her bed as the guy, cleaned the floor.

After Rosemarie and Jonathan had left, Cynthia pulled Teri's covers up and tucked her in. She looked at her roommate's pasty face, which had been so pretty at the beginning of the evening.

"The next time you invite me out for a little fun," she whispered to her unhearing friend, "remind me how much fun you had tonight, OK?"

CASE STUDY

Questions

1. Can you sympathize with Cynthia in the above account? If so, why? If not, why not?

2. What do you think Cynthia's statement, "I'm not my mommy's little girl anymore," reveals about her state of mind?

3. What factors do you think are motivating Cynthia to reconsider her behavior?

4. Do you think Cynthia is approaching her decisions subjectively or objectively? What standard(s) is she using to decide what the "right" decision would be?

5. If you were in Cynthia's shoes, would you act similarly or differently?

BIBLE STUDY PASSAGE

bible study passage

2 Samuel 11:2-18,26-27; 12:1-18

One evening David got up from his bed and walked around on the roof of the palace. From the roof he saw a woman bathing. The woman was very beautiful, and David sent someone to find out about her. The man said, "Isn't this Bathsheba, the daughter of Eliam and the wife of Uriah the Hittite?" Then David sent messengers to get her. She came to him, and he slept with her. (She had purified herself from her uncleanness.) Then she went back home. The woman conceived and sent word to David, saying, "I am pregnant."

So David sent this word to Joab: "Send me Uriah the Hittite." And Joab sent him to David. When Uriah came to him, David asked him how Joab was, how the soldiers were and how the war was going. Then David said to Uriah, "Go down to your house and wash your feet." So Uriah left the palace, and a gift from the king was sent after him. But Uriah slept at the entrance to the palace with all his master's servants and did not go down to his house.

When David was told, "Uriah did not go home," he asked him, "Haven't you just come from a distance? Why didn't you go home?"

Uriah said to David, "The ark and Israel and Judah are staying in tents, and my master Joab and my lord's men are camped in the open fields. How could I go to my house to eat and drink and lie with my wife? As surely as you live, I will not do such a thing!"

Then David said to him, "Stay here one more day, and tomorrow I will send you back." So Uriah remained in Jerusalem that day and the next. At David's invitation, he ate and drank with him, and David made him drunk. But in the evening Uriah went out to sleep on his mat among his master's servants; he did not go home.

In the morning David wrote a letter to Joab and sent it with Uriah. In it he wrote, "Put Uriah in the front line where the fighting is fiercest. Then withdraw from him so that he will be struck down and die."

So while Joab had the city under siege, he put Uriah at a place where he knew the strongest defenders were. When the men of the city came out and fought against Joab, some of the men in David's army fell; moreover, Uriah the Hittite died.

Joab sent David a full account of the battle.

When Uriah's wife heard that her husband was dead, she mourned for him. After the time of mourning was over, David had her brought to his house, and she became his wife and bore him a son. But the thing David had done displeased the LORD.

The LORD sent Nathan to David. When he came to him, he said, "There were two men in a certain town, one rich and the other poor. The rich man had a very large number of sheep and cattle, but the poor man had nothing except one little ewe lamb he had bought. He raised it, and it grew up with him and his children. It shared his food, drank from his cup and even slept in his arms. It was like a daughter to him.

"Now a traveller came to the rich man, but the rich man refrained from taking one of his own sheep or cattle to prepare a meal for the traveler who had come to him. Instead, he took the ewe lamb that belonged to the poor man and prepared it for the one who had come to him."

David burned with anger against the man and said to Nathan, "As surely as the LORD lives, the man who did this deserves to die! He must pay for that lamb four times over, because he did such a thing and had no pity."

Then Nathan said to David, "You are the man! This is what the LORD, the God of Israel, says: I anointed you king over Israel, and I delivered you from the hand of Saul. I gave your master's house to you, and your master's wives into your arms. I gave you the house of Israel and Judah. And if all this had been too little, I would have given you even more. Why did you despise the word of the LORD by doing what is evil in his eyes? You struck down Uriah the Hittite with the sword and took his wife to be your own. You killed him with the sword of the Ammonites. Now, therefore, the sword shall never depart from your house, because you despised me and took the wife of Uriah the Hittite to be your own.'

"This is what the LORD says: Out of your own household I am going to bring calamity upon you. Before your very eyes I will take your wives and give them to one who is close to you, and he will lie with your wives in broad daylight. You did it in secret, but I will do this thing in broad daylight before all Israel.' "

Then David said to Nathan, "I have sinned against the LORD."

Nathan replied, "The LORD has taken away your sin. You are not going to die. But because by doing this you have made the enemies of the LORD show utter contempt, the son born to you will die."

After Nathan had gone home, the LORD struck the child that Uriah's wife had borne to David, and he became ill. David pleaded with God for the child. He fasted and went into his house and spent the nights lying on the ground. The elders of his household stood beside him to get him up from the ground, but he refused, and he would not eat any food with them.

On the seventh day the child died.

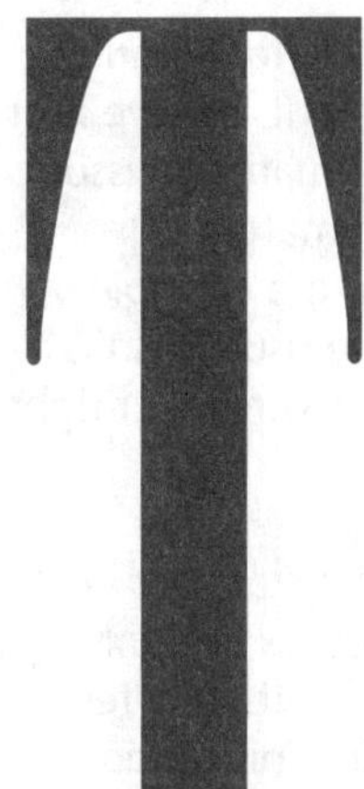

To be honest, the right choice is not always the easiest; in fact, if immoral behavior held no promise of reward or gratification, we'd have no trouble doing the right thing, would we? If it were not easier to surrender to passion and lust than to resist them, we would have no trouble avoiding sexual sin. If it were not more satisfying in some ways to badmouth a former "friend" who let us down, we wouldn't have to struggle to control our tongues.

The truth is, if we make choices simply on the basis of what will bring immediate pain or gain, the wrong choice will often be the most attractive. Of course, that's nothing new; it's been that way for centuries.

Read

As a group, carefully read 2 Samuel 11:2-18, 26-27; 12:1-18a.

Discuss

1. What choice did David face in verses 2-4?

2. What factors do you think influenced his decision? (discuss each)
   - ❑ Bathsheba's beauty
   - ❑ the gain of instant gratification
   - ❑ the pain of postponing pleasure
   - ❑ Bathsheba's marital status
   - ❑ his own marital status
   - ❑ David's loneliness
   - ❑ her money
   - ❑ her cleanliness
   - ❑ her husband's extended absence

3. Did David experience immediate gain as a result of his choice? If so, what? Discuss.

4. Did David experience long-term pain as a result of his choice? If so, what? Discuss.

5. Applying the "test of truth" to the choice David faced (in vs 2-4), discuss whether he made the right choice. Explain your conclusion.

Reflect

1. Review the choices you have made today. Did you choose immediate gratification? Why or why not?

2. Think of five or more situations this week in which you were faced with a moral choice, a choice to do right or do wrong.

3. In those situations, did you choose immediate gratification:
   - ❑ all of the time
   - ❑ most of the time
   - ❑ about half the time
   - ❑ hardly ever
   - ❑ never

4. Since wrong choices so often seem to promise immediate rewards, why would a person ever make the right choice?

Pray

Pray "Today's Prayer" (on this page) in unison.

Verse to Remember

The right choice is not always the easiest, nor the most immediately satisfying; but it is always "for your own good" (Deuteronomy 10:13).

Today's Prayer

(In Unison) Father, we live in a world of fast food, instant coffee, rapid transit, and 30-second sound bites. We have been conditioned to seek and expect immediate gratification. We're not very good at postponing satisfaction for better long-term benefits. Help us to develop that skill, and to exercise it for our own good, with the help of Your Son, through the power of the Holy Spirit, Amen.

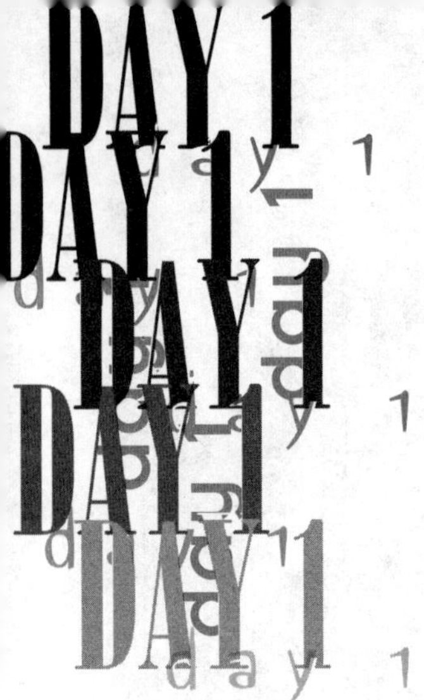

The issue of relativism versus absolutes may make for stimulating discussions and debates in college dorms, but, believe it or not, the problem of right and wrong is not primarily an issue of the mind; it is really an issue of the will. Ultimately, our struggles about right and wrong come down to a struggle between *our* way and *God's* way. The real issue usually isn't, "What's right and what's wrong?" but "Whose version of right and wrong will I accept — my own or God's?"

Even when an individual accepts the need for a standard — and even when that person acknowledges God as the only objective, universal, and constant standard of truth — a tension still exists between our will and God's will. This tension was revealed in Cynthia's vow that she was no longer her "mommy's little girl." It surfaces in the tendency (even when mental assent is given to biblical truth) to explain why God's commands don't apply *to us,* at least not in *this* situation. This tension can even be seen in the biblical record of the first man and woman.

Read

Read Genesis 3:1-23.

Study

1. Notice how, despite the tempter's deceit, the fundamental issue Eve faced in these verses was not "What's right and what's wrong?" but "Whose version of right and wrong will I accept — my own or God's?" Note the serpent's strategy.

• **The serpent persuaded the woman to doubt God's precept.** Write the verse below in which the tempter planted doubt in Eve's mind about the reasonableness of God's command.

• **The serpent prompted the woman to doubt God's person.** Write the serpent's words below that planted doubt in Eve's mind about God's truthfulness.

• **The serpent induced the woman to doubt God's motivation.** Write the serpent's words below that planted doubt in Eve's mind about God's motivation.

2. Look again at Genesis 3:6-10, 23. According to these verses, what were the first results of Adam and Eve's rebellion? (check all that apply)

- ❑ they got food poisoning
- ❑ they experienced guilt and shame for the first time
- ❑ they invented applesauce
- ❑ they were kicked out of the garden
- ❑ they damaged their relationship with God
- ❑ they lost their purity, innocence, and happiness
- ❑ they decided never to trust a snake again

3. Look at Genesis 3:11-13. The man and the woman had similar reactions when God asked them what they had done...they tried to blame someone else.

Whom did Adam try to blame? ______________________________

Whom did Eve try to blame? ______________________________

Verse to Remember

"Ah, Sovereign LORD, you have made the heavens and the earth by your great power and outstretched arm. Nothing is too hard for you" (Jeremiah 32:17).

Reflect

- Not much has changed since Adam and Eve. The devil still tries to get us to doubt God's precepts, His person, and His motivation. We still suffer unhappy consequences from wrong choices. And we try to explain our wrong choices by:

  - blaming someone else
  - explaining that it really wasn't wrong in our case
  - saying, "I didn't know it was wrong"
  - claiming, "I had no choice"

What do you think of those explanations? Do they work? Why or why not?

- What does it mean when the Bible says that God is sovereign?

> When you flee temptations don't leave a forwarding address. Now flee from youthful lusts, and pursue righteousness, faith, love and peace, with those who call on the Lord from a pure heart.
> *2 Timothy 2:22 NAS*

Apply

- Satan — in the guise of a serpent — convinced Eve that it wouldn't be so bad to reject God's version of right and wrong in favor of her own customized version. Do you ever make that mistake?

- Are you willing to **admit** that God is the only righteous judge, and that He alone can decide right and wrong?
  ❑ Yes ❑ No

Are you ready to **submit** to His version of right and wrong and follow what He says is right?
❑ Yes ❑ No

If your answer to both questions was yes, you're ready to take the following steps of submission.

1. *Turn from your selfish ways (repent and confess your sin) and admit that God is God (1 John 1:9).* Acknowledge that you have been living contrary to God's ways, that you have been trying to "do your own thing" and go your own way. Agree that your own way is wrong, and that God (and God alone) defines what is right and wrong.

2. *Submit to God as Savior and Lord and commit to His ways.* Hand your life over to Him, and depend on Him for the power to make right choices. A simple, heartfelt prayer such as the following, can open your soul to the love and light of God.

Lord Jesus, I want to know You personally. Thank You for dying on the cross for my sins. Forgive me of my sins. I trust You as my Savior and Lord. Thank You for giving me eternal life. Take control of my life. By the power of the Holy Spirit, make me the kind of person You desire and help me to make the kind of choices You want. Amen.

If you have previously trusted Christ for salvation, but you've been rejecting God's authority and trying to decide right and wrong on your own, the following prayer is suggested:

Father God, I acknowledge that I have been directing my life and that, as a result, I have sinned against You. I now invite Christ to again take His place on the throne of my life. By the power of Your spirit I commit to Your ways. Amen.

Trusting God to fill you with his Spirit doesn't mean that you will never again blow it. But you can live more consistently if you admit God is sovereign of your life, submit to His loving authority…and employ a simple process we will be discussing through the rest of this week.

Pray

Pray the prayer on this page.

Today's Prayer

O great and powerful God, whose name is the Lord Almighty, great are Your purposes and mighty are Your deeds. I submit today to Your sovereign power, and Your authority, which is Yours alone, to declare what is true and right. Amen.

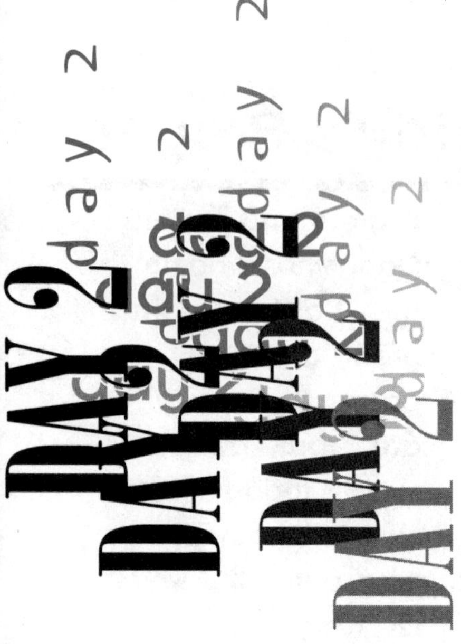

Most of us, if we were honest, would have to admit to trying to navigate the moral maze of life with less care and forethought than we give to trying to do our laundry. Do you remember the first time you did your own laundry (or are you still giving it to Mom once a month)? If you did it yourself, you carefully studied the various dials and settings, pausing to think ahead every time you were faced with a choice: hot or cold water; large or small load; regular, knits, or permanent press.

But we don't often do that in life.

A grad assistant asks if you completed last week's reading assignment, and you don't give it a thought. You answer yes, even though you'd barely begun the reading.

Your roommate tells you some juicy gossip about your resident advisor, and you don't give it a thought. You repeat it to the next person you see.

You're out on a date for the first time in a long time, and you find yourself in a dark, secluded place. You don't give it a thought. You surrender to the mood of the moment.

Every one of those "little" choices, however, represents a choice between the right path and the wrong path. Every decision represented an opportunity to select God's way or your own way. That's why the first step in the 4Cs process of submitting to God is to **consider the choice.** To consider the choice means to stop and ask yourself, "Who determines what is right or wrong in this situation?" It means to remind yourself that your choice is not between what you think is right and what you think is wrong; it's between what is objectively right and what is objectively wrong — regardless of what you think.

Read

Read Genesis 39:1-10, the story of Joseph and Potiphar's wife.

Study

1. Based on the biblical account, change the following statements to make them correct.

a. God blessed Andujar's household because of Joseph (v. 5).

b. Potiphar's wife noticed Joseph because he took steroids (vv. 6-7).

c. Joseph responded to his master's wife without thinking (vv. 7-9).

d. Joseph accepted the advances of Potiphar's wife because, he said, "no one is greater in this house than I am" (vv. 8-9).

e. Joseph had trouble seeing which choice would be right and which would be wrong (vv. 8-9).

f. Joseph had to face this temptation and make this choice once (v. 10).

2. Do you think Joseph considered the choice carefully? Or do you think he just made a decision suddenly, without any deliberation?

3. What part of the passage (Gen. 39:1-10) supports your answer?

Apply

• When you are faced with a moral choice, do you see it as a choice between going your way or God's way?

❑ Yes ❑ No ❑ Sometimes

• Do you tend to consider the choice carefully or do you make a decision suddenly, without thinking?

apply

• What can you do in the future to consider the choice between your way and God's way?

Verse to Remember

"Show me your ways, O LORD and teach me your paths; guide me in your truth and teach me, for you are God my Savior, and my hope is in you all day long" (Psalm 25:4-5).

Today's Prayer

God my Savior, please show me Your ways and teach me Your paths. Help me, as a result of this study, to submit my choices and decisions to You, and to let Your truth guide me and teach me, in the name of Jesus Christ I pray, Amen.

Pray

Read "Verse to Remember" (on this page) and then pray "Today's Prayer," making those words truly the prayer of your heart.

pray

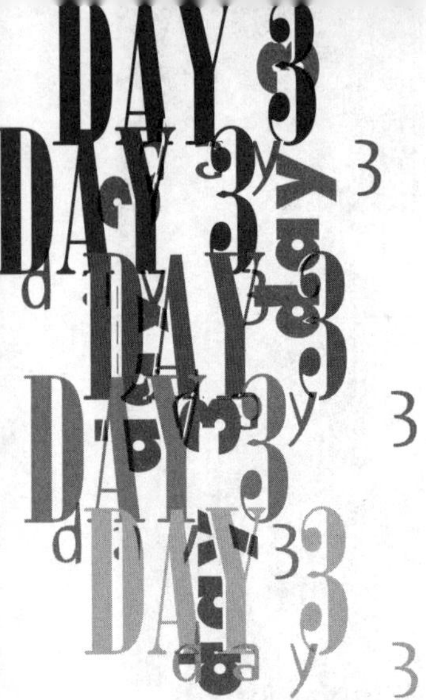

So you've admitted God's authority, and sincerely submitted to Him and His "version" (the only true version) of right and wrong. You've even begun to **consider the choice.**

You've made the first step in daily submitting your will to God and following His ways. The next step in the 4Cs process — after considering the choice — is to **compare it to God.**

In other words, after you weigh the choice you're facing in any situation, and acknowledge that it is a choice between what is objectively right and what is objectively wrong, you can then proceed to compare your choice of action to the person of God.

For example, when you flip through the cable channels and discover a steamy sex scene, you (1) **consider the choice,** recognizing it as an opportunity for a right or wrong decision, and (2) **compare it to God.**

When your sweetheart calls you from back home and asks if you've been dating anyone else, you (1) **consider the choice,** recognizing it as an opportunity for a right or wrong decision, and (2) **compare it to God.**

When a waitress incorrectly totals your lunch tab, saving you just enough cash to buy your mom a card on the way home, you (1) **consider the choice,** recognizing it as an opportunity for a right or wrong decision, and (2) **compare it to God.**

> It would be hard to pinpoint exactly when American society began referring to desserts as "sinful" and divorce as "no-fault."
> In changes so gradual that they seem revolutionary only in retrospect, classical Christian ideas about sin — like long lines at confessionals and preachers fierily challenging their congregations to mend their ways — have fallen by the wayside in many churches.
> *"What happened to Christian notions of sin?", by David Briggs (The Birmingham News, 1/7/95)*

How do you compare it to God? By using the truth process you learned last week. Write below the three key words that express that process.

P_______________
P_______________
P_______________

read

Read

Turn again to Genesis 39:1-12. Read those verses again.

understand

Understand

Joseph lived an estimated two to three hundred years before the Ten Commandments were given to the nation of Israel; however, his attitudes and actions reveal a strong knowledge of the precepts, principles, and person of God.

study

Study

1. Compare Joseph's situation with the Ten Commandments (Exodus 20:1-17). Which **precepts** would have applied to Joseph's situation?

2. What godly **principles** would Joseph have violated if he had given in to Potiphar's wife?

3. In what ways was Joseph's behavior (toward Potiphar, toward Potiphar's wife, toward God Himself) like the **person** of God?

4. What part of the Scriptural account indicates that Joseph did, in fact, compare his action to the person of God? (circle one)

(a) Joseph's statement, "No one is greater in this house than I am" (v. 9)

(b) Joseph's statement, "How then could I do such a wicked thing and sin against God?" (v. 9)

(c) Joseph's refusal even to hang around Potiphar's wife (v. 10)

(d) Joseph's action in running from the house without his cloak (v. 12)

Verse to Remember

"Trust in the LORD with all your heart and lean not on your own understanding; in all your ways acknowledge him, and he will make your paths straight" (Proverbs 3:5-6).

Review

review

• The first two steps in the 4Cs process of submission to God are:

c______________________________

c______________________________

Seems simple, eh? It's not hard to remember. Of course, doing it is another matter.

Apply

apply

• Are you facing any choices right now to which you can apply these first two steps?

❑ Yes ❑ No

• If you answered yes, complete the following statements aloud:

If I look at this particular situation as an opportunity for doing what is objectively right or wrong, I would...

If I compare this particular action to the person of God, I would...

Pray

pray

Spend a few moments in prayer, perhaps using the following as a guideline.

Today's Prayer

Lord of heaven and earth, I marvel at Your greatness and Your goodness. Help me to trust in You with all my heart, and to acknowledge You every day by comparing every decision to Your nature and character, in Jesus' name, Amen.

• Talk to God honestly about the statements you've made above.

• Ask Him to give you patience and perseverance as you continue in this study.

• Pray for your needs and concerns, and for those of your friends and loved ones.

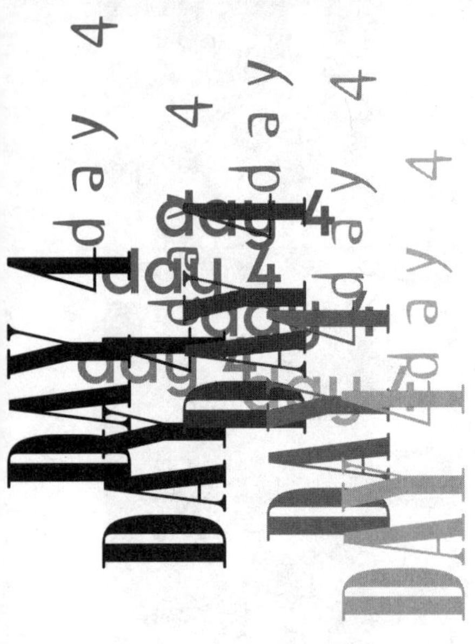

What were your family vacations like as a kid? Did your dad pack you, your three brothers, and seven sisters, into a Ford station wagon for a drive across the Mojave Desert in July— with no air conditioning? Or maybe you spent every summer vacation with your cousin Elmer, who picked his nose and collected rocks. It could have been worse, you know; at least your dad wasn't Doctor Oxnard, the geology professor who has 25 years' worth of slides of his poor kids posing in front of rock formations all over God's green earth.

Whatever your vacation experience, your family probably got lost once or twice, right? When that happened, how long did your dad drive around aimlessly before finally stopping to ask for directions? An hour? Two hours? A week and a half?

Well, we don't have to stumble around the moral maze until we see a gas station. God has already given us directions, in the form of precepts that point to principles that spring from His person. Yet, incredibly, we often choose to go our own way rather than follow directions from someone who knows the way.

For that reason, even when we **consider the choice** and **compare it to God,** we still must **commit to His way.** Once we have compared our selfish desires to God's absolute standard, we must choose between our way and God's way. We must consciously turn from our selfish ways and resolutely commit to God's way.

> I know God will not give me anything I can't handle. I just wish that He didn't trust me so much.
> —*Mother Teresa*
>
> *from Do It! by John-Roger and Peter McWilliams (© 1991 Prelude Press, Inc., California)*

Read

Carefully and thoughtfully read again Genesis 39:1-12.

Study

1. Based on your reading of the above Scripture passage, answer the following questions by circling T for true or F for false.

T F Joseph had to face the temptation posed by Potiphar's wife many times

T F Joseph didn't think what she had in mind was wrong; he just didn't find her attractive

T F Joseph refused to go to bed with Potiphar's wife, but he still hung around with her

T F Joseph's behavior shows that he was committed to obeying God

T F Joseph committed to God's way because it was convenient

T F Committing to God's way apparently meant to Joseph that he would try to do the right thing

Reflect

• Joseph did the right thing in the face of unremitting temptation because he **considered the choice** (recognizing that his situation involved a choice between what was objectively right and what was objectively wrong, regardless of his situation), **compared it to God** (recognizing that sexual involvement with Potiphar's wife would have contradicted the nature and character of a God who is pure, faithful, and trustworthy), and **committed to God's way**, deciding that he would accept God's directions and adjust his behavior accordingly. Not only that, but verse ten makes it clear that he planned his behavior to help him commit daily to God's way.

Courage is doing what you're afraid to do. There can be no courage unless you're scared.
—*Eddie Rickenbacker*

from Do It! by John-Roger and Peter McWilliams (© 1991 Prelude Press, Inc., California)

Apply

apply

• Are you ready to commit to God's way? It's the kind of commitment you make once, and then make again every time you're faced with a moral choice. It means turning from your selfish ways and saying, "God, I see that Your way is right, and I commit to following You, with Your help, in the power of Your Holy Spirit."

• Why not put your commitment in writing, a kind of "manifesto," to guide you in your future decision-making. Your commitment should include the following steps.

> "I will **CONSIDER** my choices carefully. I will **COMPARE** my attitudes and actions to God and His Word. I will turn from my selfishness that causes me to look for excuses to justify my behavior. I will **COMMIT** to God's ways. I will allow God's Holy Spirit to empower me to make right moral choices.

Get the idea? Use the lines below to record your prayer to God— your own "manifesto," for making right choices.

____

____

____

____

____

Powerless
"Men may spurn our appeals, reject our message, oppose our arguments, despise our persons, but they are helpless against our prayers."
— *J. Sidlow Baxter*

Pray

• You may be discovering that your own moral decision-making has lacked one or more of these elements we've been discussing. If that's the case, take a few moments to confess that lack (and any effects it has had on your life and on the lives of your loved ones) to God. Surrender to Him, and ask for His healing and restoration in specific areas.

Today's Prayer

God and Father, draw my heart toward You today. Increase my faith in You and my love for You, so that I will desire to please You in all that I do, in all that I think, in all the choices that I make. I pray these things in the name of Jesus, who did Your will, Amen.

pray

Once you have considered the choice, compared it to God, and then committed to God's way, there is one final step in the process of submitting to the Sovereign Lord, and that is to Count on God's Protection and Provision.

When we humbly admit God's sovereignty and sincerely submit to His loving authority, we can not only begin to see clearly the distinctions between right and wrong, but we can also begin to **count on God's protection and provision.**

This doesn't mean that everything will be rosy; in fact, God says pretty bluntly that you may sometimes suffer for righteousness' sake. But even such suffering has rewards. Living according to God's way (and allowing the Holy Spirit to live through you) brings many spiritual blessings, like freedom from guilt, a clear conscience, the joy of sharing Christ, and (most importantly) the blessing of God upon your life.

You can also enjoy many physical, emotional, psychological, and relational benefits when you commit to God's ways. While God's protection and provision should not be the primary motivation for obeying God, it certainly provides a powerful encouragement for choosing right and rejecting wrong!

Anyone who is actually following a recognized road will not be too worried if he hears non travellers telling each other that no such road exists.
J. I. Packer,
Knowing God, pg. 15

Read

Read Genesis 39:13-20.

read

Study

1. Based on the above account, what would you say were the immediate results of Joseph's choice? (check all that apply)

❑ He was disgraced and imprisoned
❑ He earned a guest appearance on "The Tonight Show"
❑ He was falsely accused of wrongdoing
❑ He lost the trust of his dean of students
❑ He accepted a position with a powerful government lobbying firm

study

2. Do these accounts make it sound like Joseph enjoyed rewards for choosing to do right?

❑ Yes ❑ No

Verse to Remember

"If the LORD delights in a man's way, he makes his steps firm; though he stumble, he will not fall, for the LORD upholds him with his hand" (Psalm 37:23-24).

3. Do you think the consequences of his actions made him sorry he had committed to God's way?

❑ Yes ❑ No

Why or why not?

4. "Oh great," you may say. "What an endorsement for submitting all my decisions to God! I can hear my friends now: 'Commit to God's way, get falsely accused of a terrible crime, go to prison — where do I sign up?'" Well, now, hold on just a minute. That's not the end of the story. Remember, doing the right thing may not bring immediate rewards. But did Joseph suffer in the long run for committing to

God's ways and following His directions? Let's see. Read Genesis 39:21-23. What was Joseph's experience in prison?

5. Do you think the integrity he displayed in his former position helped him earn the prison warden's confidence?

❑ Yes ❑ No

Why or why not?

6. Read Genesis 41:38-52. What benefits did Joseph eventually enjoy as a result of God's protection and provision? (check all that apply)

❑ wisdom	❑ free cable
❑ integrity	❑ power
❑ a new car	❑ wealth
❑ a good reputation	❑ a wife and children
❑ a gold watch	❑ paid holidays
❑ authority	❑ a clear conscience
❑ the favor of men	❑ the favor of God

Review

review

There you have it'...the 4Cs for submitting every moral decision — not just daily, but hourly — to the Sovereign Lord who knows you, who knows the future, and who knows what's best. Close your eyes and see if you can remember each of the 4Cs. Then check your memory and see how well you remembered these steps.

Apply

apply

• Do you have trouble understanding any of the 4Cs?

❑ Yes ❑ No

If so, which one? ________________________

• Do you have trouble remembering any of the 4Cs?

❑ Yes ❑ No

If so, which one? ________________________

• Do you have trouble following any of the 4Cs?

❑ Yes ❑ No

If so, which one? ________________________

Pray

pray

Pray "Today's Prayer" (on this page).

Today's Prayer

Sovereign Lord, I admit Your sovereignty; I submit to Your authority; I commit to follow Your ways. I trust You to uphold me with Your hand, and I will count on Your protection and provision, even when it isn't obvious, even when it isn't immediate...In Jesus' name, Amen.

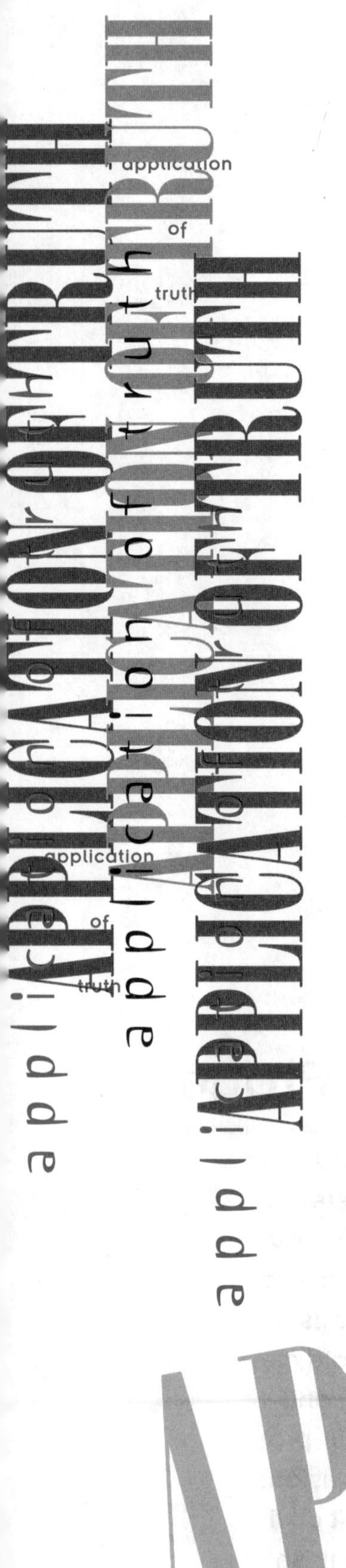

To what degree do you think your moral decisions are influenced by your emotions, by your moods? Do your emotions tend to rule your intellect, or the other way around? What effect might your temperament have on your success in using the 4C process? How can you use your temperament to your advantage? Involve your friends in helping you discover ways to capitalize on your strengths and compensate for your weaknesses.

• Play the "instant gratification" game. Each time you see a sign or ad touting "fast service" or "Spee-D Results," picture a scale such as the one below:

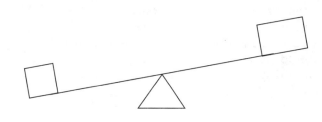

With the scale in your mind, determine whether speed of result (instant gratification) and quality of result (long-term benefit) are compatible in the advertised product. Also ask yourself which you would choose. Be sure to relate your mental exercise to the short-term "pain"/long-term "gain" that often characterizes right choices.

• Use your shoes as a memory device. Do you remember trying to learn to tie your shoes when you were a preschooler? Probably not, but it was a difficult task made up of several steps. You had to practice and practice in order to master the multi-step process, yet today you tie your shoes without even thinking about the steps. How come? Because you've done it so often it's automatic! You may be thinking that you'll never stop and do all that 4Cs stuff every time you're faced with a moral decision...But it's like tying your shoes. Just as that process has become second nature to you, the 4Cs can become second nature, an almost automatic process for making right choices. The key, of course, is practice (you'll get plenty of that in the coming weeks of study). This week, quickly review the 4Cs (**consider the choice, compare it to God, commit to God's way, count on God's protection and provision**) every time you tie your shoes.

APPLICATION

• If you're musical, try composing a chorus, rap, or commercial "jingle" for the 4Cs process ("Here's a little song/About the choice of right from wrong…"). Or adapt the words to fit a favorite tune. Use your musical creation to help you remember — and practice — the 4Cs.

• Consider obtaining one of those "5-D" posters or postcards to place on your wall or in a notebook as a visible means of expressing the change that is occurring in your truth view, the way you're seeing things differently as a result of this study and your new understanding of God as the source of truth. Use it as a conversation starter to introduce your friends to the truth.

APPLICATION

Notes from Session Four

Notes from Session Four
notes from session four
Notes from Session Four
notes from session four
Notes from Session Four
notes from session four
Notes from Session Four
notes from session four
Notes from Session Four
notes from session four
notes from session four
notes from session four
notes from session four

1. I have the following questions...

2. I have the following concerns...

3. Because of this session, I feel...

Hear a whisper in the night
See a distant burning light
That you cannot explain
Oh, you try to shut it out
Cover it up with all your doubts
But it won't go away
Answer the call, answer the call

Got a knock upon the door
Getting loud, you can't ignore
A voice is calling your name
Don't you live in the status quo
Don't you go where you always go
It's crying out for change
Answer the call, answer the call

Call it inspiration, call it revelation
call it anything at all
But burning deep in you
Is something you have gotta do
So answer, answer the call

Now the path is there to take
Now the choice is there to make
Don't let the vision fade
You'd be living in the dark
Running away from your own heart
If you just turned away
Answer the call, answer the call
It may be the inner city
Maybe your own family
The mission field may lie in you
But you know the Word is true
And it's staring back at you
So answer, answer the call

The message is for you
So whatever you do
Answer, answer the call

White Heart's "Answer the Call"
Words and Music by Mark Gersmehl, Billy Smiley

RANDOM ACTS OF HONESTY

WEEK FIVE

"Honesty is praised," wrote Juvenal, the first-century Roman poet and satirist, "and starves." What did he mean? He meant that everyone praises honesty, but few practice it.

Miguel de Cervantes (the author of *Don Quixote*) wrote, "Honesty's the best policy." If that's true, however, why does honesty seem so rare, not only to Juvenal, but to us?

The philosopher Immanuel Kant proclaimed what is called the "categorical imperative." When determining whether something was the right thing to do, Kant posed the question, "What would happen if everyone were required to do what you are considering doing?"

Let's ask this question about honesty. What kind of world would we have if everyone were required to be completely honest in all situations?

First of all, somebody would get offended...

- Your Aunt Sylvia would get offended when you told her the truth about that mushroom casserole that she baked for your graduation dinner.
- Your sister would get offended when you told her what you really think about her new hairstyle.
- Your friend would get offended when you told him that his idea for the homecoming float was incredibly stupid, grossly expensive, and was done by the Kappas last year.

But beyond these offenses, what would the world be like? Well...

...you could trust the mechanic when she told you the "synchro-digital, compu-quadratic auto-bobble" in your new car needed replacement.

...you could trust the dealer who sold you your car to tell you if there was something wrong with your "synchro-digital, compu-quadratic auto-bobble."

...you wouldn't have to put $50 worth of chains and locks on your bike when leaving it alone for five minutes.

...you could share an idea with a co-worker without worrying if he or she would claim it for his or her own.

> Truth carries with it confrontation. Truth demands confrontation; loving confrontation, but confrontation, nonetheless.
>
> *Francis Schaeffer, The Great Evangelical Disaster, pg. 64*

There is a lot that could be said for such a world. Unfortunately, you and I don't live in such a world. We experience dishonesty in as many forms as individuals can devise—and the number is growing. Cheating, stealing, lying...in one form or another, we have all been victims (and unfortunately, perpetrators) of these forms of dishonesty.

Why is honesty praised? Why is it a virtue? What makes it right?

And what makes it so uncommon?

THE SCENE ON CAMPUS

the scene on campus

In 1992, $882 million worth of computer equipment was stolen, according to Safeware, a Columbus, Ohio, insurance company specializing in computer coverage. That was a 10 to 12 percent increase over 1991, and the figure was expected to have climbed again in 1993...
And once stolen, the equipment moves fast. A hot PC changes hands three to five times in the first 24 hours, and another five to eight times in the second 24 hours...

PC World, February 1994
"A Nation of Liars," by Merrill McLoughlin with Jeffery L. Sheler and Gordon Witkin (U.S. News & World Report, 2/23/87)

CASE STUDY

Cynthia smiled to herself as she walked down the hall toward her dorm room. She felt better than she had in weeks. She had just attended her first campus Bible study, and had met eight other Christians. It was just the first meeting, but she felt optimistic that the small group would develop into a close circle of friends, and she felt the need for friends very keenly right now. She opened the door to her room and fumbled to find the light switch.

She flipped the lights on, and was startled to see Teri sitting on her bed, her knees drawn up to her chest and her face buried in her knees.

"Teri?" Cynthia whispered. Her roommate didn't move. "Teri, are you all right?"

Teri lifted her head to reveal a face streaked with tears.

"What's wrong?" Cynthia asked. She deposited her Bible on her own bed and stepped gingerly to Teri's side of the room. She propped herself on the edge of Teri's bed.

Her roommate sniffled and wiped her nose with the back of her hand. Cynthia popped up from her position, fetched a handful of tissue from the box on the desk, and offered it to Teri.

"Are you all right?" she repeated. "Do you feel like talking?"

Teri wiped her eyes, and then fastened them warily on Cynthia.

"I need your help," she said.

"Sure," Cynthia agreed immediately. "What is it?"

Teri dabbed her eyes again and inhaled deeply. "I have to go to court," she said. I was cited for underage drinking." She lifted the tissue to her face and blew her nose. She looked at Cynthia, then dropped her gaze to the tissue in her hands. "I don't even remember getting it," she sobbed, nodding at the pink slip of paper beside her on the bed. "I wasn't thinking too clear that night."

"What can I do?" Cynthia asked.

"I need you. I need you to say I was here...with you."

Cynthia's mouth closed suddenly. A long, heavy silence seemed to blanket the room. Neither spoke.

Finally, Cynthia broke the silence. "You want me to lie." It wasn't a question.

"No," Teri answered hastily. "No, it's just that I need a friend. I wouldn't ask you if it wasn't important. I just need you to back up my story."

The two roommates fell silent again. Cynthia swallowed and licked her lips as if trying to rid her mouth of a bad taste. This was her chance to be a friend to Teri; it could be the beginning of a great friendship — or a bitter feud.

"Please..." Teri pleaded.

Why do students cheat?

- stress
- competition, specifically competition for admission into graduate schools, for scholarships, and for jobs after graduation
- social climate of cheating by authority figures (parents, teachers, business executives, and government officials) creates indifference to cheating
- viewed as a legitimate means for getting ahead and coping with stress

"Academic Dishonesty Among College Students," by Sheilah Maramark and Mindi Barth Maline (Issues in Education, August 1993)

Questions

1. How is Teri justifying what she's asking Cynthia to do?

2. How is Cynthia approaching her choice?

3. What do you think Cynthia should do? Why?

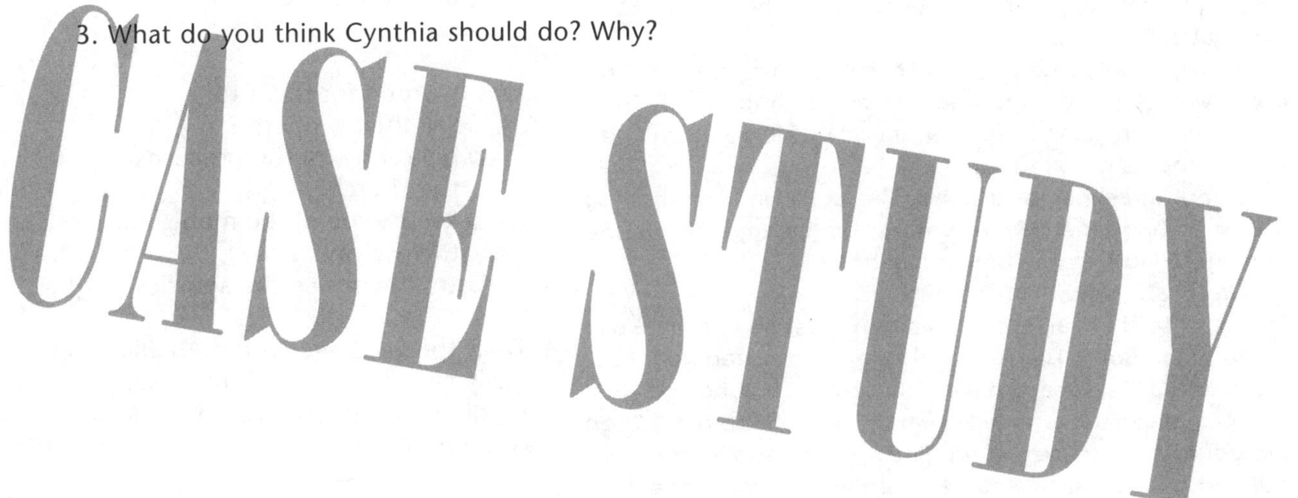

BIBLE STUDY PASSAGE

> "The public sees a clever dodge as no different than someone telling you a fat, bald lie. The politician sees it as a rule of the game."
>
> *Christopher Matthews, former House staffer "A Nation of Liars," U.S. News & World Report, 23 February 1987, 55.*

Research indicates that one of the areas in which young adults struggle most is the area of honesty. Two of every three (66 percent) say they have lied to a "parent, teacher, or other older person" within the last three months. Slightly fewer — six in ten (59 percent) — say they have lied to a friend or peer within the last three months. More than one-third (36 percent) admit that they have cheated on an exam or other evaluation within that same three month period, and nearly one-sixth (15 percent) say they have recently stolen money or other possessions.

Such deceit and dishonesty are characteristic of those who embrace (whether they know it or not) a "man-centered" view of truth, one that relies on human ideas — rather than divine standards — of truth and morality. Over half (52 percent) of the young adults in evangelical Christian churches are struggling with this issue; they tend to believe that "lying is sometimes necessary."(*RFW*, p.169)

Acts 4:32-5:11

All the believers were one in heart and mind. No-one claimed that any of his possessions was his own, but they shared everything they had. [3]With great power the apostles continued to testify to the resurrection of the Lord Jesus, and much grace was upon them all. There were no needy persons among them. For from time to time those who owned lands or houses sold them, brought the money from the sales and put it at the apostles' feet, and it was distributed to anyone as he had need.

Joseph, a Levite from Cyprus, whom the apostles called Barnabas (which means Son of Encouragement), sold a field he owned and brought the money and put it at the apostles' feet.

Now a man named Ananias, together with his wife Sapphira, also sold a piece of property. With his wife's full knowledge he kept back part of the money for himself, but brought the rest and put it at the apostles' feet.

Then Peter said, "Ananias, how is it that Satan has so filled your heart that you have lied to the Holy Spirit and have kept for yourself some of the money you received for the land? Didn't it belong to you before it was sold? And after it was sold, wasn't the money at your disposal? What made you think of doing such a thing? You have not lied to men but to God."

When Ananias heard this, he fell down and died. And great fear seized all who heard what had happened. Then the young men came forward, wrapped up his body, and carried him out and buried him.

About three hours later his wife came in, not knowing what had happened. Peter asked her, "Tell me, is this the price you and Ananias got for the land?"

"Yes," she said, "that is the price."

Peter said to her, "How could you agree to test the Spirit of the Lord? Look! The feet of the men who buried your husband are at the door, and they will carry you out also."

[1]At that moment she fell down at his feet and died. Then the young men came in and, finding her dead, carried her out and buried her beside her husband. Great fear seized the whole church and all who heard about these events.

Read

Carefully read Acts 4:32 - 5:11 as a group.

Discuss

1. Were Ananias and Sapphira required to sell their property and lay all the proceeds at the apostles' feet?

2. What do you think motivated Ananias and Sapphira to sell their property and give a portion to the church?

3. Was it wrong for them to:
   - ❑ sell their property?
   - ❑ give some of the proceeds to the church?
   - ❑ keep some of the money for themselves?
   - ❑ try to deceive the apostles?

4. Does the Scripture record Ananias actually lying? If he didn't tell a lie, what did he do that was so bad? What was the result?

5. Does the Scripture record Sapphira actually lying? What was the result?

6. To what standard does Peter refer in rebuking Ananias (vv. 3, 4)?

7. If everyone who ever lived were placed in one of these three circles, where would you place Ananias and Sapphira? Write their names in the appropriate circle. Where would you place Peter the apostle? Write his in the appropriate circle. Barnabas (of Acts 4:36)? The men who carried out the bodies of Ananias and Sapphira? Yourself? What names would you place in the circle on the left? What names would you place in the circle on the right?

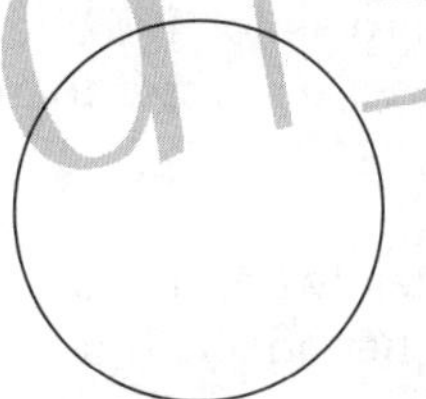
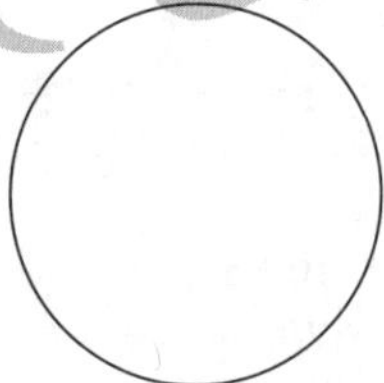

People who never lie | People who sometimes lie | People who always lie

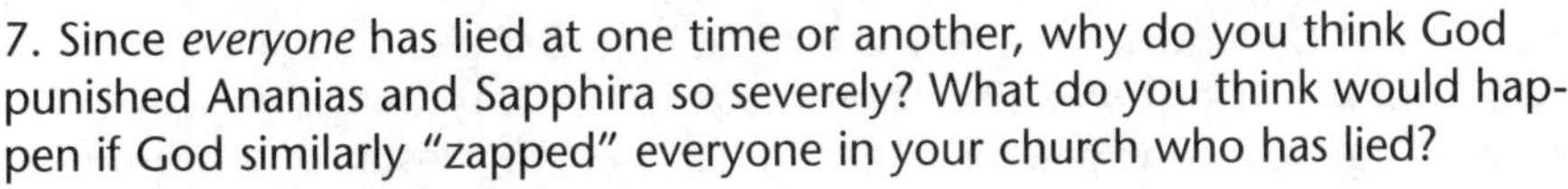

7. Since *everyone* has lied at one time or another, why do you think God punished Ananias and Sapphira so severely? What do you think would happen if God similarly "zapped" everyone in your church who has lied?

8. If everyone does it, how can you say that dishonesty is wrong?

Point to Remember

Honesty is not only the best policy; it's the right one, too.

Apply

• Does the experience of Ananias and Sapphira bring to your mind any changes that need to happen in your life? Circle any of the forms of dishonesty which need to get out of your life.

Lying — Deception — Stealing — Cheating

Lying by Silence — Plagiarism — Taking undeserved credit

"Borrowing" and not returning items — Pretending not to know

Avoiding paying income or other taxes — Falsifying financial aid forms

____________________ — ____________________

This little light of mine, I'm gonna let it shine…
—*children's song*

Today's Prayer

(Responsively) We praise You, God, and we thank You for all You've done; We know that You test the heart and are pleased with integrity. Help us not only to value honesty, but to live it, too, with the help of Your Son, through the power of the Holy Spirit , Amen.

• If God is revealing the presence of some of these things in your life, confess them and determine to avoid any future involvement with them. God will enable you if you need the strength.

Pray

Pray "Today's Prayer" (on this page) responsively.

The decision Cynthia faces in "The Scene on Campus" may seem simple to you. Her roommate has asked her to back up her story. She can either agree or refuse.

But to Cynthia, it's not that simple. She has many conflicting interests and emotions. How is she supposed to balance her hunger for acceptance and friendship with her desire to tell the truth? What if she were to lie for Teri and it was discovered? What if there were other witnesses there who contradicted what Cynthia said?

But if she were to refuse, Teri would certainly be mad at her. She probably would never speak to her again, and Cynthia might never make any friends on campus. Besides, the Christian thing to do would be to help her friend, wouldn't it?

To complicate matters, Cynthia must make a decision in a few seconds. She doesn't have time to check a Bible concordance and read through a workbook on right choices. That's usually the way things are. Decisions about right or wrong are most often the result of a moment's thought or a split-second impulse.

Verse to Remember

"So give your servant a discerning heart to govern your people and to distinguish between right and wrong" (1 Kings 3:9).

Still, an amazing number of thoughts and impulses take place in that short amount of time (such as all those conflicting considerations mentioned above). If the human mind can process all that information in seconds, it can certainly handle the 4Cs process. In fact, the 4Cs process can actually streamline your decision-making, because it sorts all the various impulses and thoughts that assail your mind in a moment of decision.

So let's apply the 4Cs process to Cynthia's decision.

Ultimately, the real "usefulness" of the Christian faith...depends on the conviction that the faith is not so much useful as true.
Os Guiness, The American Hour, pg. 379

Think Thru

1. So far, Cynthia is evaluating the rightness or wrongness of her action based on the immediate benefits each alternative offered. That's only natural, of course. What are some of the short-term benefits Cynthia might enjoy as a result of backing up Teri's story?

2. What are some short-term consequences she might face if she doesn't agree to Teri's request?

3. Now for an important question: do those considerations help her determine which decision is right?

❑ Yes, because

❑ No, because

Cynthia must be careful not to judge right and wrong (which is objective) by her *experience* (which is subjective). She must not let her situation cloud her perception of right and wrong.

The first step in making right choices — **consider the choice** — is so important, because it can immediately clear a mind clouded by a confusing and unpleasant situation. It can remind you that your choice is not between what you think is right and what you think is wrong; it's between what is objectively right and what is objectively wrong — regardless of what you think.

Today's Prayer

Merciful God, I admit that I often make moral decisions based on what I think, or on what will have the quickest benefits to me. Help me from this day on, when I am faced with a choice, to first consider the choice as a choice, not between what I think is right or wrong, but between what is objectively right and what is objectively wrong — regardless of what I think. I pray this, knowing that it is only possible through Your Holy Spirit's power, Amen.

Read

Read 1 Kings 3:5-10.

Study

1. The central request of King Solomon's prayer, in verse 9, was for "a discerning heart" that would enable him to do two things. What are those two purposes Solomon cites?

... to ____________________

... to ____________________

2. Do you think Solomon's prayer affirms a belief in an objective, universal, and constant standard of right and wrong?

❑ Yes ❑ No

Reflect

• Why do you think Solomon asked for the ability to distinguish between right and wrong?

• How could Cynthia benefit from Solomon's example? What would it mean for her to consider the choice in her current situation?

Apply

• How could you benefit from Solomon's example?

Pray

Close today's study time in prayer, meditating on 1 Kings 3:9 and reaffirming God's authority as the Source of right and wrong.

If Cynthia were to stop long enough to consider the choice, she would recognize that the choice she faced — whether to "back up Teri's story" — was not between what she thought was right or wrong, but between what was right or wrong, independently of her particular situation. If she were to pause just long enough to remind herself that neither she nor her situation has the power to determine what is right or wrong, she would take a major step in clearing her thinking, in making her way through the moral maze.

She could then have proceeded to the next step in making right choices. What would happen if Cynthia were to **compare her choice** to the nature and character of God? What might she learn by tracing her choice through precept and principle to the Person of God?

Study

1. ***Precept***

• Read Leviticus 19:11. How do those precepts apply to Cynthia's situation?

• Read Jesus' response to the rich young ruler's question about eternal life in Mark 10:19 and complete the phrase that applies to Cynthia's situation:

> *"You know the commandments: 'Do not murder, do not commit adultery, do not steal, do not give false testimony, do not ___________, honor your father and mother.' "*

• Read the following verses and then write the two-word phrase that appears in each verse: 1 Timothy. 3:8; Titus 1:7,11.

• How do those verses apply to Cynthia's situation?

The apostles asserted that Christ alone is the truth in the midst of a world that was more religiously diverse than any we have known in the West until relatively recently.
David F. Wells,
No Place for Truth, pg. 104

2. ***Principle***

• What positive principle do you think lies behind each of those precepts? In other words, what attribute does God want us to possess that such behavior would contradict? (Hint: Proverbs 12:22 refers to this principle.)

3. ***Person***

• What is it, then, about God that the precepts and the principle point to? Is there something in God's nature and character that would make Cynthia lying for Teri to be wrong? Read the following Bible verses and complete the statement that follows.

2 Samuel 7:28 God is _______________

John 3:33 God is __________________

Psalm 31:5 God is the God of _________

Reflect

• If Cynthia were equipped with the 4Cs instead of the confusing and competing thoughts and feelings prompted by her situation, she would be able to see that to lie would be wrong, regardless of how much she wants friends, regardless of how much she wants to help Teri, regardless of how Teri might respond to her refusal. Lying would be wrong because, if you compare it to God, you will discover that:

- God's precepts forbid dishonest gain
- God's precepts forbid dishonest gain because God values honesty and trustworthiness
- God values honesty and trustworthiness because God is trustworthy and true

Apply

• Review your recent decisions; are there any you should have applied the 4Cs to?

❑ Yes ❑ No

• How would you see things differently if you **consider the choic**e in that situation and **compare it to God?**

Pray

Take a few moments to pray, committing that situation to God, asking Him for forgiveness (if necessary), and asking Him to guide you in future decisions through the 4Cs.

Verse to Remember

"The Lord detests lying lips, but he delights in men who are truthful" (Proverbs 12:22).

Just as grace is the "relational" aspect of God's character, truth is the structure of His character.

Henry Cloud, When Your World Makes No Sense, pg. 27

Today's Prayer

Father, the call to be like You in all I do is overwhelming. Only through the work of Your Spirit in my life can I reach that goal. Please empower me and enable me to that end. As part of that work, give me the wisdom to see the truth, the honesty to speak it, and the compassion to speak it lovingly, in the name of Jesus Christ I pray, Amen.

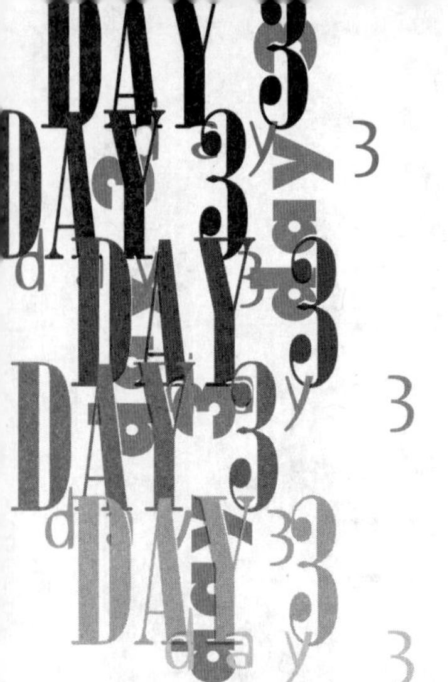

Even if Cynthia were to admit God's authority by **considering the choice** and objectively determined the rightness or wrongness of the action she's considering by **comparing it to God,** she's not home free. It still remains for her to **commit to God's way.**

Think Thru

1. What might committing to God's way involve for Cynthia in her current situation? (check all that you think apply)

- ❑ a quick prayer to God
- ❑ a long prayer to God
- ❑ ask God for a sign
- ❑ tell Teri, "you made your bed, now lie in it"
- ❑ agree to Teri's plan
- ❑ feign sickness
- ❑ feign death
- ❑ suggest Teri just tell the truth
- ❑ agree to go with Teri, but not to lie for her
- ❑ offer to visit Teri in "the Big House"
- ❑ share the "Four Spiritual Laws" with Teri
- ❑ resolve to do the right thing if it benefits her
- ❑ resolve to do the right thing regardless of the benefits or consequences

think thru

2. If Cynthia is to make the right choice, she must *admit* that her choice is a choice between a real right and a real wrong, *submit* to God as the authority who determines what is right or wrong, and *commit* to God's way by conforming to what God says is right, regardless of the benefits or consequences.

Verse to Remember

"Trust in the Lord with all your heart and lean not on your own understanding; in all your ways acknowledge him, and he will make your paths straight" (Proverbs 3:5-6).

Read

read

Read Matthew 26:36-46.

Understand

After celebrating the Passover with His disciples, Jesus went to the Garden of Gethsemane, just across the Brook Kidron from the temple and the fortress where He would soon be tried and crucified. Some scholars state that the Kidron, which Jesus would have crossed to get to Gethsemane, probably flowed with the blood from the many lambs slaughtered that day as Passover sacrifices. The sight and smell of that vivid reminder of His approaching sacrifice may have contributed to the urgency of Jesus' statement to His disciples in verse 38 and His prayer in verses 39 and 42.

Study

study

1. In the space below, compare and contrast the decision Jesus faced in the Garden of Gethsemane with Cynthia's choice (in "The Scene on Campus"). How are they different? How are they similar?

Differences:

Similarities:

2. Briefly compare and contrast how Jesus responded to the decision He faced with the way Cynthia approached her choice.

Differences:

Similarities:

Reflect

• Do you think Jesus let his situation dictate His decision? If so, in what way? If not, how did He prevent that mistake?

• Why did Jesus refer to His coming passion as "this cup?"

• Why didn't Jesus just tell the Father what He wanted and then claim the answer to His prayer?

• What does Jesus' attitude and approach to decision-making in these verses indicate, in relation to truth?

Apply

• Can you think of any situation in your life that would have ended differently if you had committed to God's way? If so, describe it here:

• Have you already committed to submitting to God, either in your college or young adult group or during your daily sessions in this workbook?

❑ Yes ❑ No

Today's Prayer

Lord of heaven and earth, I marvel at your greatness and Your goodness. Help me to trust in You with all my heart, and to acknowledge You every day by comparing every decision to Your nature and character, in Jesus' name, Amen.

Pray

• If you have already made such a commitment, renew it now, perhaps repeating the "manifesto" you composed (on page 85) as a closing prayer to God.

• If you have not made such a commitment, why not do so now? Admit God's sovereignty, and submit your will to Him, using the steps on pages 79.

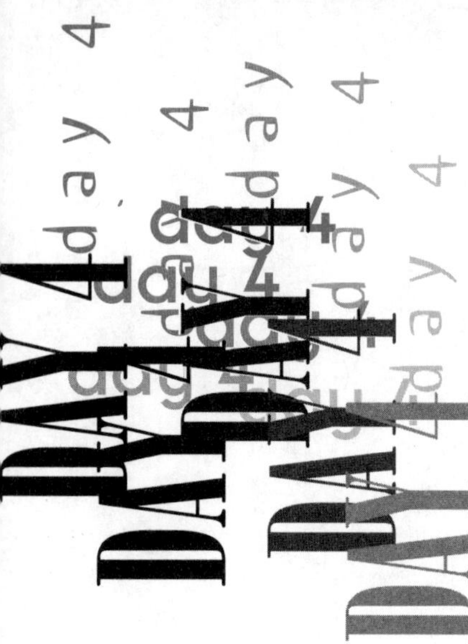

Once an individual considers the cost, compares it to God, and commits to God's way, there is yet one final component of the 4Cs, and that is to **count on God's protection and provision.**

God's commandments are like an umbrella. When you put up an umbrella, it shields you from the rain. But if you choose to move out from under that umbrella during a storm, you're bound to get wet.

As long as you stay under the umbrella of God's commands, you'll be shielded from many unpleasant and tragic consequences. However, if you step out from under that protective cover, you should not be surprised if you suffer the consequences.

Once you have committed to God's ways, you can then look forward to the benefits of that umbrella.

Think Thru

1. What kinds of protection might Cynthia enjoy if she were to make the right choice?

2. Cynthia may not instantly realize any of the benefits of making the right choice, but if she commits to God's ways and then count on His loving protection and provision, even thanking God in faith before she sees any fruits of her obedience, she will pave the way for a much happier and healthier future.

Study

1. Why is that true? Because *God's standard of honesty protects from guilt.* Guilt is among the most powerful of emotions, and it will cling to the dishonest heart like a python, choking the life out of its victim. The psalmist David realized that, and expressed it in Psalm 38:4. Read that verse and copy it below.

If Cynthia were to commit to God's way, she would be protected from the burden of guilt that would result from lying for her friend.

2. *God's standard of honesty protects from shame.* What might happen if Cynthia backs up Teri's story, and is caught in the lie? Even if she isn't caught, would Teri have any reason to respect her roommate? Fill in the missing words to Proverbs 13:5.

> *The righteous hate what is ______________, but the*
>
> *wicked bring ______________ and ______________.*

3. God's standard of honesty protects from entrapment in a cycle of deceit. To repeat Solomon's wise words, "A fortune made by a lying tongue is a fleeting vapor and a deadly snare" (Proverbs 21:6). It is a snare because every lie breeds more lies, every deceit leads to more deceit. Like a person who paints himself into a corner, the dishonest heart is soon trapped by its own duplicity. Cynthia would be foolish to believe that she would have to lie once for Teri; she would probably have to repeat the lie (perhaps to Teri's parents, for example), and may be called on to "cover" for her friend again. Adherence to God's standard of honesty would save her from being snared in a web created by her own deceit.

4. God's standard of honesty protects from ruined relationships. Cynthia may think that lying for Teri may pave the way for friendship, but a relationship that is created by a lie is headed for ruin. Trust is the very foundation of relationship, and trust simply can't survive in the atmosphere of deceit.

Verse to Remember

"Therefore each of you must put off falsehood and speak truthfully to his neighbor, for we are all members of one body" (Ephesians 4:25).

Reflect

• Can you think of any other ways that Cynthia might be protected by adhering to God's standard of honesty?

• If obeying the precepts of God protects us from so much harm, why do so few people do it?

> Do not be quick in spirit to be angry or vexed, for anger and vexation lodge in the bosom of fools.
> *Eccelesiastes 7:9 AMP*

Apply

• Do you doubt any of the above claims regarding God's standard of honesty? If so, why? If not, why not?

• When's the last time you told the truth in a difficult situation (when it might have been "easier" to lie)? Are you sorry you did so? Why or why not?

• Are you facing any decisions now in which you need to count on God's protection? Have you already considered the choice and committed to God's way?

Today's Prayer

Heavenly Father, I trust You because You have never lied. Help me to earn that kind of trust from my friends and loved ones, as I depend on Your grace and strength, and count on Your loving protection, through Jesus my Lord, Amen.

Pray

• Spend a few moments meditating on the "Verse to Remember" (on this page) and then pray "Today's Prayer."

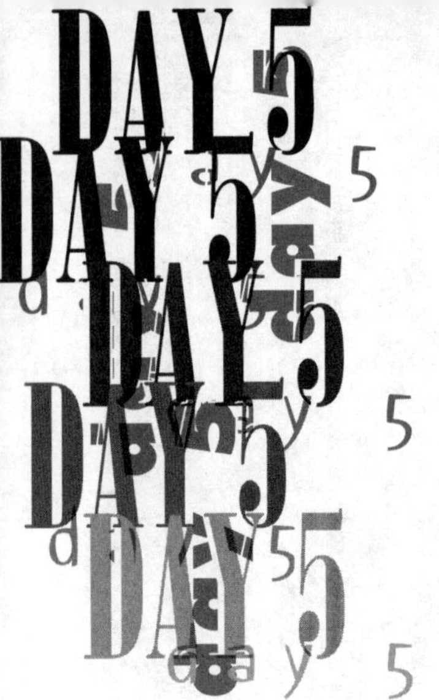

As he did in the garden of Eden, the Tempter, our adversary, makes it his business to prompt us to doubt or forget that "Every good and perfect gift is from above, coming down from the Father of the heavenly lights, who does not change like shifting shadows" (James 1:17).

Like Cynthia, we are vulnerable to the lie that dishonesty will somehow work our good; but "every good and perfect gift is from above, coming down from the Father."

We tend to think that a lie can somehow promote our welfare; but "every good and perfect gift is from above, coming down from the Father."

We entertain the absurd notion that sin may somehow be in our best interests; but "every good and perfect gift is from above, coming down from the Father."

God, who promises to protect and provide for us, has never failed to keep His promises. The man or woman who considers the choice, compares it to God, and commits to God's way will not only experience God's protection, but also His provision.

Read

Read Genesis 22:1-19.

Understand

Abraham lived in the midst of a culture in which many people worshiped gods who demanded child sacrifice. So, while God's instruction in verse 2 may have been terrible to Abraham's ears (especially since it seemed certain to negate God's earlier promise of Genesis 17:5-6), it would not have been unbelievable.

Verse to Remember

"Test me, O LORD, and try me, examine my heart and my mind; for your love is ever before me, and I walk continually in your truth" (Psalm 26:2-3).

Study

1. Do you think Abraham expected his obedience to God's command to result in protection and provision?

❑ Yes ❑ No

2. In what ways did God provide for Abraham as a result of his obedience?

3. In what ways might God provide for Cynthia if she, like Abraham, were to commit to God's ways regardless of the apparent benefits or consequences?

4. Did you mention the fact that God's standard of honesty provides a clear conscience, and an unbroken relationship with God? If Cynthia were to lie for her roommate, she would have damaged her walk with God. On the other hand, with every right choice, she preserves and enriches that relationship.

5. God's standard of honesty provides a reputation for integrity. Cynthia may not realize it, but every time she makes the right choice, she is building a reputation. Choosing God's way builds a reputation for integrity. Read Proverbs 22:1 and copy its words below:

6. God's standard of honesty provides trust in relationships. If Cynthia were to agree to Teri's plan, Teri may some day reason: "If she lied for me, how do I know she won't also lie to me?" But a strong foundation of trust will improve and enrich the quality of a person's relationships, providing something that money can't buy, and dishonesty can't achieve.

Swallowing angry words before you say them is better than having to eat them afterwards.

God's Little Instruction Book II

From the fruit of his mouth a man's stomach is filled; with the harvest from his lips he is satisfied. The tongue has the power of life and death, and those who love it will eat its fruit.

Proverbs 18:20,21

Reflect

• Has your perspective on Cynthia's situation changed since you first read "The Scene on Campus?" If so, in what way? If not, why not?

• Do you think Cynthia's appraisal of her situation would changed if she were to think through the 4Cs? If so, in what way? If not, why not?

Review

• Write the four steps of the 4Cs from memory below.

C____

C____

C____

C____

Apply

• What do you think would happen if you began now to choose God's way and count on His protection and provision? (check all that apply)

- ❑ He would disappoint me
- ❑ He would make me miserable
- ❑ He would protect me
- ❑ He would embarrass me in front of my friends
- ❑ He would provide for me
- ❑ He would make me sorry I trusted Him

• Is anything keeping you from admitting God's sovereignty, submitting to His authority, and committing to His ways? If so, what? How can you overcome that? Can you enlist the help of another person?

• If you have not done so already, begin now to implement the 4Cs process in your decision-making. Share your efforts — your struggles and successes with a close friend.

Pray

Thoughtfully and sincerely search your heart and test your thoughts; then pray "Today's Prayer" (on this page), which is based on Psalm 26:2-3).

Today's Prayer

Test me, O Lord, and try me today. Examine my heart and mind, and help me to be honest with You and with myself today. Your love is ever before me, and I thank You because Your motivation is always to protect me and provide for me. I want to walk continually in your truth. Overcome all the obstacles in my heart and mind and let me submit to You completely, and commit to Your way, not my own, in Jesus' name, Amen.

APPLICATION

Cynthia contemplated giving up her integrity to receive "friendship." She's not alone. A lot of people are willing to trade things in order to get friendship. Draw a line down the center of a piece of note paper. On the left, list the things you are willing to "trade" in order to make a friend. On the right side, list the things you refuse to trade for friendship. Keep the list in a textbook or Bible where you are likely to come across it every once in a while.

• Play the "What If" game with a friend (especially when you're waiting for a bus, or waiting in line at the cafeteria). Take turns imagining how the world would be different if everyone were absolutely honest. Answers might include not locking our bikes, not chaining things down, not installing alarm systems, not paying theft insurance. The "What If" game can help you see how, even on an individual level, God's standard of honesty protects and provides for you.

• Often when we say someone has a "reputation," it has a negative connotation. Who do you know that has the reputation for being honest, a person of integrity, a "person of his (or her) word?" Talk with this person about how he or she came to have this reputation. Thank them for the example they provide for others.

• Have you seen those bumper stickers touting "Random Acts of Kindness?" Make an effort to notice (and practice) "random acts of honesty." Congratulate your friend for his refusal to copy computer programs for others. Point out your roommate's extra effort to return a borrowed book when she said she would. Applaud your little sister for giving Mom and Dad the change she didn't use for last week's skating party. And, as much as possible, use each instance to review *why* such honesty is right.

• The next time you read a newspaper or magazine, keep an eye out for any "correction" notices. Where do these notices usually appear? What does the placement of these corrections say about the paper's perspective on honesty? Do the corrections you and I make to our mistakes have a similar perspective?

Notes from Session Five

1. I have the following questions...

2. I have the following concerns...

3. Because of this session, I feel...

LOVE PROTECTION
WEEK SIX

Love, it has been said, is a universal language. It is extolled everywhere, by everyone, as the pinnacle of virtue. "What the world needs now," Dionne Warwick sang, "is love, sweet love." The Beatles claimed, "All you need is love." Michael Bolton contended, "Love is a wonderful thing."

But what is "love"? Is it just a "second-hand emotion," as Tina Turner sang? Is it accurate to say that you "love" your pony or your cat? Is it appropriate to say you "love" chocolate or you "love" volleyball? Are those things different from your "love" for your parents? And is that "love" different from your "love" for a girlfriend or boyfriend?

Of course, if you really want to understand a word, it's always good to start with a dictionary. Most dictionaries list ten or more definitions of "love!" The first definition usually says love is a strong, complex emotion or feeling causing one to appreciate, delight in and crave the presence or possession of another and to please or promote the welfare of the other.

Did you notice that there are two distinct facets of this definition? The first facet is the "emotion," or feeling which most people associate with the word "love," that sense of excitement, nervousness, or exhilaration that human beings identify as "love."

But the second facet goes beyond just feeling "all gooey inside." "To please or promote the welfare of the other" requires an act of the will; in fact, it may or may not even involve emotion. The first part of the dictionary definition reflects how one feels; the second part, "to please or promote the welfare" of another person is far more objective. It involves doing.

Such a concept of love is very different from the "love" our culture promotes. But it sounds strikingly similar to the love Jesus commanded.

> LOVE & SECURITY: Have you noticed that when you deeply love a man and he deeply loves you, and you feel completely secure in each other's love, you don't have to laugh at his jokes unless they're funny?
>
> *LOVE & GUILT & THE MEANING OF LIFE, ETC. by Judith Viorst (Simon & Schuster, Inc., New York, 1979)*

An expert in the Law of God once came to Jesus with a question. He was a Pharisee, a group of people who knew the commandments inside and out; in fact, they believed that there was a commandment to cover every detail of life.

"Teacher," the man said, "which is the greatest commandment in the Law?"

Jesus answered, "'Love the Lord your God with all your heart and with all your soul and with all your mind.' This is the first and greatest commandment. And the second is like it: 'Love your neighbor as yourself.' All the Law and the Prophets hang on these two commandments" (Matthew 22:36-40).

In other words, Jesus was saying that everything God has revealed to us about right and wrong — all the dos and don'ts of His commandments, all the shalts and shalt-nots — are simply explanations and amplifications of His command to love.

Sounds good, of course, but what does it mean in "the real world?" That is the focus of your discoveries and decisions this week as you continue applying the 4Cs process to the choices and challenges you and the people all around you must face every day.

Those who indulge in perversion tell those who are living normal lives that it is they who are deviating from what is natural. They think they are following a natural life themselves. They are like people on a ship who think it is those on the shore who are moving away. Language is relative everywhere. But we need a fixed point by which to judge. So the harbor is that fixed point for those who are moving aboard the ship. But in morality, where are we going to find a harbor?

Blaise Pasca

THE SCENE ON CAMPUS

CASE STUDY

Cynthia stopped abruptly, just before the door to her room slammed in her face.

She saw me coming, Cynthia thought, and *she slammed the door like that on purpose.* Her roommate Teri had been treating Cynthia cruelly for the last four days, ever since Cynthia had refused to lie at Teri's upcoming court appearance for underage consumption of alcohol.

"I can't say what you want me to say," Cynthia had told her roommate. "I couldn't lie like that, Teri, but I will go to court with you."

"I can't believe it," Teri had answered through tear-filled eyes. "You think you're so good, don't you?"

Cynthia opened her mouth to protest, but Teri kept talking, her voice becoming louder with each word, until she was shouting. "Well, let me tell you something — you make me sick! You act like you're some kind of special Christian or something, and then you turn your back on a friend." Cynthia opened her mouth again, but Teri cut her off before she had a chance to speak a word in her own defense. "I don't need your help," she said.

Since that horrible scene of a few days ago, Teri hadn't spoken a civil word to her roommate, and it seemed to Cynthia as if the popular Teri had succeeded in turning the whole student body of State University against her. She had noticed people staring at her and whispering about her in the cafeteria, and it seemed like the people in the dorm were shunning her.

She pushed the door open and stepped into her room. Teri, who was sitting cross-legged on her bed with a textbook open on her lap, suddenly slammed the book closed and reached for her towel and bath robe.

"I'm going to take a shower," she muttered bitterly, as if Cynthia's entry into the room made studying impossible. "I need to wash off some secondhand scum."

She slammed the door on her way out, and Cynthia was left alone in the room that had, in the past four days, become more like a cell than a home. She stood in the middle of the room, frozen by a combination of rage and loneliness, when a knock sounded at the door.

She opened the door and saw Rosemarie, the young woman she had met at orientation. Cynthia smiled and opened the door wide.

Rosemarie seemed to look beyond Cynthia into the room. "Is Teri here?" she asked.

Cynthia's smile faded. "No. She's in the shower."

Rosemarie waved a pink slip of paper in the air, as if trying to come to a decision. Finally, she sighed and extended the paper to Cynthia. "Would you give this to her?"

Cynthia slowly took the piece of paper from between Rosemarie's fingers.

"I was on desk duty downstairs this afternoon," Rosemarie explained. "And this message came in. I just got off the desk, but I've got to go." She seemed to hesitate, and glanced at the paper. "It sounded important."

Cynthia looked at Rosemarie's writing on the paper without reading it. Finally, she shrugged. "Sure," she said.

Rosemarie thanked her, and trotted down the hall as Cynthia shut the door and lifted the message to read it. She didn't take the time to read the whole message, but she read enough to understand that Teri's court date had been moved up; it was tomorrow morning, not Friday.

A question slowly formed in Cynthia's mind: What would happen if Teri never got the message? What if Cynthia managed to "forget" to tell Teri about the change? It might complicate things for Teri. It might get her in even more trouble. It might teach her a lesson. It would certainly serve her right.

Questions

1. How do you respond to the above? Do you sympathize with Cynthia? Teri? Both? Neither?

2. Do you think Cynthia is thinking clearly? Consistently?

3. Have you ever felt like Cynthia? What were the circumstances? How did you resolve them?

4. What do you think Cynthia should do? Why?

CASE STUDY 2

BIBLE STUDY PASSAGE

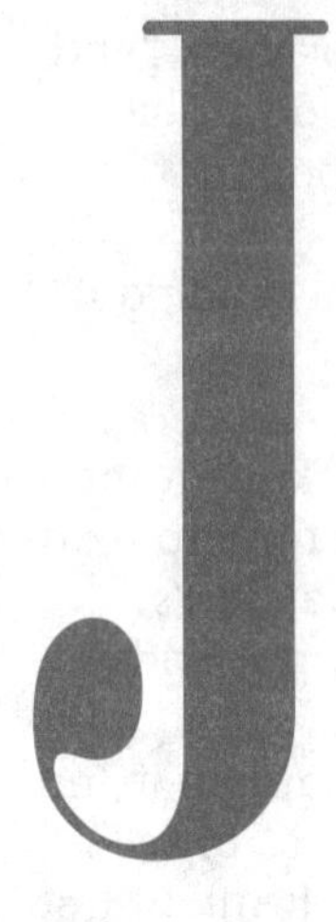

Jesus said that we are to love God with all that we have—heart, soul, mind, and strength. Does that mean that we are to have warm emotions or feelings for God? Sure it does, at least occasionally. But it also means that we are to be concerned with what God wants out of the relationship He has with us, what is important to Him — even when we don't *feel* "gushy" toward Him. It also means that we will sincerely attempt to promote God's welfare, seeking (as Jesus taught His disciples to pray), for His will to be done on earth just as it is in heaven.

Loving God is the greatest commandment, but the second is just like it: Love one another! That's where it gets sticky. Loving people is not as easy as most of us would like it to be. People are so...so...so human! They have tempers and bad habits and ugly spots. They are pretty unloveable sometimes. But remember, love is not only a feeling or emotion toward someone; it is also the action of "promoting their welfare." Promoting their welfare does not require me to please them, nor does it require me to have "warm fuzzy" feelings for them. Promoting someone else's welfare asks me to do what is genuinely good for that person, something which will benefit him or her.

You and I can love anyone. We don't have to have warm feelings for them; we don't have to please them. But to the extent that we can do what is good for them and promote their well-being, we can love them.

1 Corinthians 13:1-13

If I speak in the tongues of men and of angels, but have not love, I am only a resounding gong or a clanging cymbal. If I have the gift of prophecy and can fathom all mysteries and all knowledge, and if I have a faith that can move mountains, but have not love, I am nothing. If I give all I possess to the poor and surrender my body to the flames, but have not love, I gain nothing.

Love is patient, love is kind. It does not envy, it does not boast, it is not proud. It is not rude, it is not self-seeking, it is not easily angered, it keeps no record of wrongs. Love does not delight in evil but rejoices with the truth. It always protects, always trusts, always hopes, always perseveres.

Love never fails. But where there are prophecies, they will cease; where there are tongues, they will be stilled; where there is knowledge, it will pass away. For we know in part and we prophesy in part, but when perfection comes, the imperfect disappears. When I was a child, I talked like a child, I thought like a child, I reasoned like a child. When I became a man, I put childish ways behind me. Now we see but a poor reflection as in a mirror; then we shall see face to face. Now I know in part; then I shall know fully, even as I am fully known.

And now these three remain: faith, hope and love. But the greatest of these is love.

Warm Up

Divide the group into two teams. Using a 30 second timer (or watch with a second hand), give each team 30 seconds to sing at least eight words of a song with the word "love" in it. If they succeed, play passes to the next team, and so on, until one of the teams is stumped. (Syllables, such as "Da doo doo doo, da da da da," do not count as words, but repeated words or phrases may be counted separately).

Read

Carefully read 1 Corinthians 13:1-13.

Discuss

1. Do you think this passage refers to (check any that apply):
   - ❑ romantic love
   - ❑ parental love
   - ❑ friendship
   - ❑ familial love (within a family)
   - ❑ Christian love

❑ all of the above
❑ none of the above

2. Re-read verses 4 through 8. In the boxes below, list the things Paul says love is or does, and those things he says that love is not or does not do.

Point to Remember

Love is not only what you feel; it is also what you do.

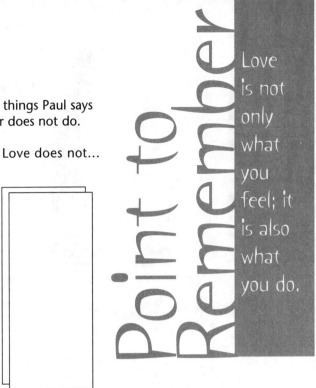

3. Are any of the lists longer than others?
❑ Yes ❑ No

4. Circle the two longest lists. Why do you think they are longer than the other two?

Apply

• How has today's study affected your understanding of "love?"

• How would you evaluate your relationships (romantic, family, friends), according to the dictionary definition in the introduction to this unit? Do you rely only on emotion, or do you also seek to please and promote the welfare of those you "love?"

Today's Prayer

Father, love is so misunderstood in the world today. Clarify in my mind and heart what it means to love someone, to love You, and to love myself. In everything I do, show me the necessity of doing it in love, and enable me, through the Spirit of Christ, to do just that, in Jesus' name, Amen.

• How would you evaluate your relationships, according to the 1 Corinthians 13 definition of love? (Are you "patient," "kind," not "envious or boastful," etc.?)

• If your answers to the previous two questions were not what you'd like them to be, how can you begin today to align your relationships with your new understanding of love?

Pray

Pray "Today's Prayer" (on this page).

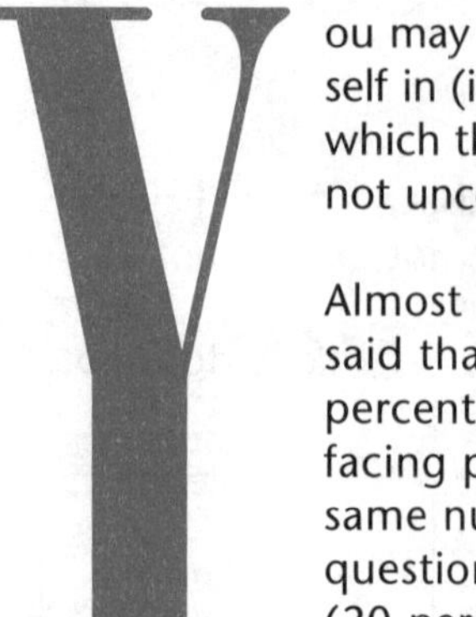

ou may never have been in the position Cynthia finds herself in (in "The Scene on Campus"). Yet the survey upon which this study is based reveals that her experience is not uncommon among young adults in the church.

Almost half (49 percent) of the individuals surveyed said that life has become too complex. Two in five (41 percent) said that they feel isolated and alone when facing personal problems or crises, and roughly the same number (38 percent) admit that they sometimes question whether life is worth living. And one in five (20 percent) admit to having tried to physically hurt someone within the past three months, while nearly one in four (23 percent) say they tried to inflict emotional hurt on another person in that same period. (*RFW*, pp.259-261.)

Of course, technically, Cynthia's not contemplating *doing* anything to Teri; she's simply choosing not to relay a phone message. There's nothing wrong with that, right? Let's see; let's apply the 4Cs process to Cynthia's action...Or *in*action.

Verse to Remember

"And now these three remain: faith, hope and love. But the greatest of these is love" (1 Corinthians 13:13).

Think Thru

1. On what basis is Cynthia evaluating the rightness or wrongness of her action? (check all that apply)
   - ❑ immediate benefits
   - ❑ an objective standard
   - ❑ long-term benefits
   - ❑ long-term consequences
   - ❑ her feelings
   - ❑ short-term consequences

2. Do you think Cynthia has some justification for her plan? What are some of the factors that may make her plan seem right?

think thru

2. What are some of the immediate benefits she might enjoy as a result of her plan?

3. Do those considerations determine which decision is right?

   ❑ Yes, because

   ❑ No, because

You see, Cynthia is trying to judge right and wrong (which is objective) by her *emotions* (which are subjective). She is letting her feelings cloud her judgment of right and wrong. Rather than justifying her actions and proclaiming them "right" because of what Teri has done to her, Cynthia would be much better off to **consider the choice,** remembering that her choice is not between what she thinks is right or what she thinks is wrong, but between what is right or wrong, regardless of what she thinks.

Read

• Cynthia is not the first to face such a tempting opportunity. The Bible tells the story of David, who had been wronged by a former friend named Saul. In fact, Saul had actually tried to kill David (See 1 Sam. 18:10-11;19:1-7).

• Read 1 Samuel 26:1-25.

Study

1. Was David's experience was similar in any way(s) to Cynthia's? If so, how?

2. Do you think David tried to judge right and wrong (which is objective) by his *emotions* (which were subjective)?

❑ Yes ❑ No

Apply

• Does your response to personal conflict typically resemble Cynthia's response? David's? Neither?

• Recall the most recent conflict you've had with another person. How did you determine what was right or wrong in that relationship? How did your emotions affect your decision?

• Are you still making choices based on the immediate benefits?

• Are you justifying decisions about what's right or wrong according to what's in it for you?

• Are you trying to judge right and wrong by your emotions?

• Or are you beginning to **consider the choice,** making choices based on a belief in an objective, universal, constant standard of right and wrong?

Pray

Conclude today's study in prayer, perhaps using "Today's Prayer" (on this page) as a guide.

Today's Prayer

God of love, thank You for Your love for me, a love that always protects, always trusts, always hopes, and always perseveres. I confess that I don't always feel loving, and I don't always act in love. Please fill me so full of Your love that it will overflow from my life to the benefit of those around me, in Jesus' loving name, Amen.

Cynthia is still trying to judge the rightness or wrongness of her actions herself. If she would stop and ask who decides what's right or wrong in this situation, she would be better equipped to recognize that her choice is between what is right or wrong objectively, regardless of her emotions or explanations. She could then proceed to the next step in making right choices, which is to **Compare it to God.** What would happen if Cynthia were to compare her action to the nature and character of God? What would she learn by tracing her choice (through precept and principle) to the Person of God Himself?

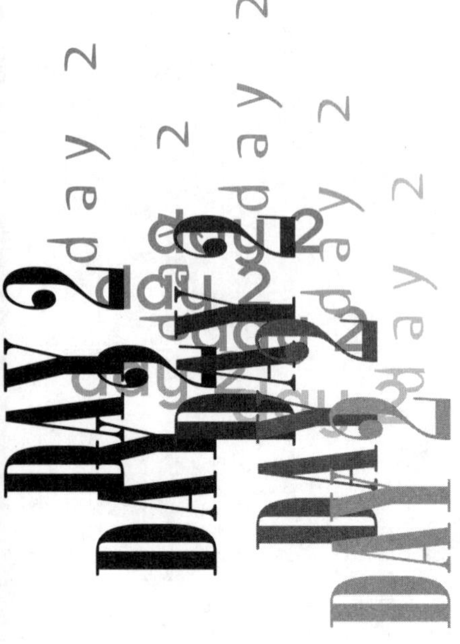

Study

1. ***Precept***

• Do you remember Jesus' words in the introduction to this unit of study? Read Matthew 22:36-40. How do you think His words apply to Cynthia's situation?

• Read Matthew 5:43-46. What precept did Jesus *quote*?

• How do you think those verses apply to Cynthia's situation?

2. ***Principle***

• What positive principle do you think lies behind each of those precepts?

3. ***Person***

• What is it, then, about God that the precepts and the principle point to? Is there something in God's nature and character that would make Cynthia's action toward Teri wrong? Read the following verses and complete the statement that follows.

1 John 4:8 God is ___________________________

1 John 4:16 God is __________________________

2 Corinthians. 13:11 God is "the God of _______"

> Man needs the answers given by God in the Bible to have adequate answers not only for how to be in an open relationship with God, but also for how to know the present meaning of life and how to have final answers in distinguishing right and wrong.
> *Francis Schaeffer, How Should We Then Live?, pg. 81*

Reflect

• God's loving nature dictates His action. Read the following Scriptures that describe the love of God. After each passage, write down a phrase or thought that summarizes how God's loving nature is manifested in action.

"The LORD did not set his affection on you and choose you because you were more numerous than other peoples, for you were the fewest of all peoples. But it was because the LORD loved you and kept the oath he swore to your forefathers that he brought you out with a mighty hand and redeemed you from the land of slavery, from the power of Pharaoh king of Egypt" (Deuteronomy *7:7-8).*

Summary:____

"Surely it was for my benefit that I suffered such anguish. In your love you kept me from the pit of destruction; you have put all my sins behind your back" (Isaiah 38:17).

reflect

Summary:____

"But because of his great love for us, God, who is rich in mercy, made us alive with Christ even when we were dead in transgressions— it is by grace you have been saved" (Ephesians 2:4-5).

Summary:____

If Cynthia were trying to judge right and wrong according to the 4Cs (instead of justifying it according to her emotions), she would be able to see that to her action would be wrong, regardless of how Teri treated her, regardless of how lonely she is, regardless of whether she could accomplish it without taking any positive action. Her action would be wrong because if you compare it to God, you discover that:

- God's precepts command us to love, and to act in love
- God's precepts command us to love because God values love
- God values love because God is love

Cynthia's attitude and action toward Teri is wrong because it is not loving. It contradicts the nature of God, who is love.

Verse to Remember

"Whoever does not love does not know God, because God is love" (1 John 4:8).

Apply

apply

- Are there any unloving attitudes in your heart and mind? Are you contemplating or pursuing any actions that are contradictory to His nature and character (as revealed through precept-principle-person)? List below any attitudes that you need to submit to God's standard of love.

my attitude toward

____

my attitude about

____

- List below any actions that you need to change, based on God's standard of love:

the way I act toward

____

the way I act when

____

Pray

pray

Close today's study with a prayer asking God to reveal to you any actions or attitudes you need to compare to Him.

Today's Prayer

Loving Father, You not only say You love me, but You have shown it by Your actions, especially in sending Your only Son to die for me. Help me, by Your Holy Spirit, to emulate You in acting in love toward others, regardless of my emotions or explanations. In the name of Jesus Christ I pray, Amen.

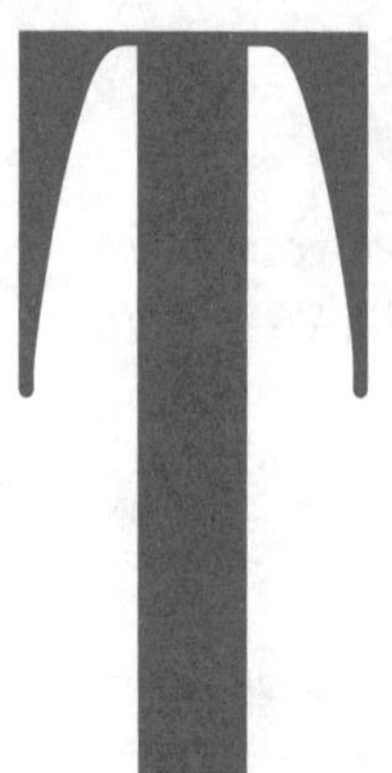

The first two steps toward making right choices require an **admission** of God's sovereignty; the third step demands **submission.** And that's where most people have trouble, because they don't *want* to turn from their own selfish ways and self-serving desires. So they find ways to justify their actions according to their individual situations, instead of submitting and committing to God's ways.

Read

Turn to 1 Samuel 26, the story of Saul and David in the Desert of Ziph. Read verses 1-8.

read

Study

1. Had Saul ever mistreated David? If so, how? (See 1 Sam. 18-20 if you need help)
   - ❑ by badmouthing him
   - ❑ by throwing things at him
   - ❑ by trying to kill him
   - ❑ by not speaking to him
   - ❑ by assigning dangerous tasks to him
   - ❑ by turning other people against him
   - ❑ by slashing the tires on his Jeep Cherokee

2. Read verses 9-13. How did David respond to Saul's mistreatment?

study

3. Read verses 14-25. *Why* do you think David responded that way?

Verse to Remember

"You have heard that it was said, 'Love your neighbor and hate your enemy.' But I tell you: Love your enemies and pray for those who persecute you, that you may be sons of your Father in heaven" (Matthew 5:43-45).

4. Read 2 Samuel 1:1-4, 17-24. How did David respond to news of Saul's death?
   - ❑ he threw a party
   - ❑ he breathed a sigh of relief
   - ❑ he lamented
   - ❑ he said, "It serveth him aright"
   - ❑ he sang a song praising Saul and Jonathan

5. Read 2 Samuel 2:1-7. How does David's action in these passages compare with God? How does it compare with Cynthia's action?

Reflect

- Do you think committing to God's way would be easy for Cynthia?

❑ Yes ❑ No

- What do you think would be hardest for her?

- Would committing to God's way mean only relaying the message to Teri or would it involve more? Would it simply involve not doing what's wrong, or would it require more of her?

Apply

- What is hardest for you about committing to God's way?

- Remember that once a person commits to God's way, however, he or she must depend on Him to provide the power to walk in His ways. All of us lack the power to consistently make right choices on our own; we need His help.

- Have you committed to His ways? Are you depending on His help?

Pray

Close today's study with a prayer renewing your commitment and thanking God for giving you the power to walk in His ways.

Today's Prayer

Father, the Bible says that You loved me when I was still in my sins, and that You love me now, even though I don't always follow Your ways. I know I can never earn Your love, but I want to respond to it by committing to Your ways today, and every day, in Jesus' name, Amen.

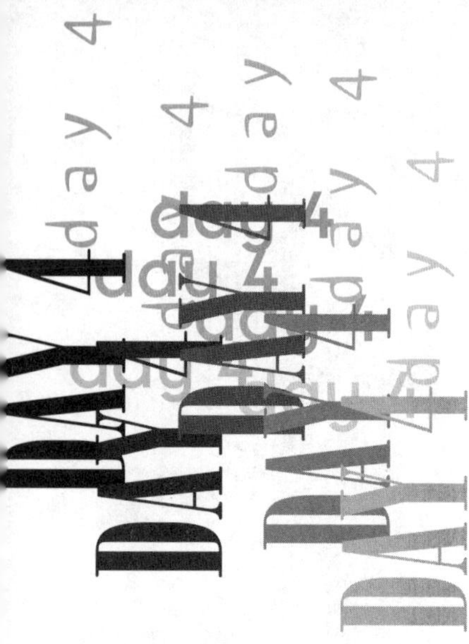

The last of the 4Cs, you'll remember, is to **count on God's protection and provision.** To be honest, however, it may be difficult to see how committing to God's way in such a mundane thing as relaying a phone message (about a court date, no less!) could possibly be the means of God's protection and provision. What possible benefits to Cynthia could there be for making the right choice in this circumstance?

Perhaps that question will be answered in today and tomorrow's study. But even if it isn't, remember that God's protection and provision shouldn't be the sole (or even the primary) motivation for obeying Him. You might say the fourth C isn't an ingredient of the "Right From Wrong cake." It is the icing.

Read

Let's learn once more about David's confrontation with Saul, the first king of Israel. Read 1 Samuel 26:21-25.

Half the nation's children are now growing up in household quite different from the "Leave It to Beaver" model, according to several 1994 reports from the Census Bureau. While 51 percent of kids still live with both biological parents, the other 32 million are being raised with a single parent, stepparents, half siblings or grandparents seated across the dinner table. That's a big shift from the '40s, '50s and '60s, when nearly 70 percent of kids had traditional families. More kids than ever — 27 percent — are being raised by a lone parent, twice as many as in 1970.

"Breakthroughs: The Feats of 1994 That Have Changed Our Lives," (U.S/ News & World Report, December 26, 1994)

Study

1. According to the biblical record in 1 Samuel 26:1-25, do you think David (check all that apply):

- ❑ considered the choice
- ❑ compared it to God
- ❑ committed to God's way
- ❑ counted on God's protection and provision

2. Copy or paraphrase the words of David that reveal that he was counting on God's protection and provision.

3. What kinds of protection might Cynthia enjoy if she were to make the right choice? She would be protected from strife, because *God's standard of love protects from strife.* Have you ever seen a willful two-year-old express his anger by biting *himself*? Such behavior illustrates the fact that hatred and hostility harms us more than anyone at whom we may aim our hatred. God knows that unloving attitudes and actions poison our own lives and fill them with strife; a life of love toward others is a life of peace.

4. Cynthia would be protected from self-centeredness, because *God's standard of love protects from self-centeredness.* Perhaps you know someone who evaluates every conversation, every relationship, every event of her life in terms of how it affects him or her. Such a person may have some friends and acquaintances without really loving any of them. Dr. S. I. McMillen, in his book, *None of These Diseases,* quotes an internationally known psychiatrist, Alfred Adler, as saying:

> *The most important task imposed by religion has always been, "Love thy neighbor..." It is the individual who is not interested in his fellow man who has the greatest difficulties in life and provides the greatest injury to others. It is from among such individuals that all human failures spring.[1]*

5. Finally, she would be protected from spiritual harm, because God's standard of love protects from spiritual barrenness. John the Apostle wrote, "Anyone who does not love remains in death. Anyone who hates his brother is a murderer, and you know that no murderer has eternal life in him" (1 John 3:14-15). Such strong language communicates the tragic spiritual consequences God wants to protect us from; that is why He commands us to love. God wants to protect us from the barrenness of an unloving soul.

Reflect

• Can you think of any other ways in which committing to God's way of love might protect Cynthia?

reflect

Apply

• Complete the following statements aloud...

"One relationship I need to submit to God's standard of love is..."

"One way I need to be more loving in my relationships with others is..."

"One way I way I will do that this week is to..."

apply

Verse to Remember

"Dear children, let us not love with words or tongue but with actions and in truth" (1 John 3:18).

Today's Prayer

My Lord and my God, I ask You, please, to show me today and in the weeks to come the many ways You protect me, especially as I am obedient to Your commands through the strength and Spirit of Jesus. Amen.

Pray

• Spend a few moments meditating on the "Verse to Remember" (on this page) and then pray "Today's Prayer."

pray

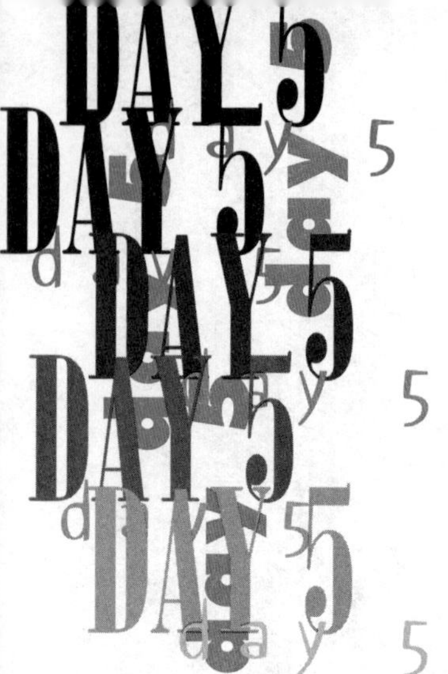

The test of truth reveals that love is right because it reflects the nature and character of God Himself, who is holy and righteous. The evidence of truth (that is, the evidence of God's loving motivation) reveals that love is also beneficial.

Read

Read Hosea 1:2-9;3:1-5.

Understand

Though the text is not explicit, it is apparent that sometime after her marriage to Hosea, Gomer became unfaithful to her husband (in fact, the name Hosea gave to her third child, meaning "not my children," may have referred to Israel's and Gomer's unfaithfulness. The text also makes it clear that at some point Gomer left Hosea, lived with another man, and engaged in prostitution.

Study

1. How do you think Gomer's unfaithfulness would have made Hosea feel? (check all that apply)

- ❑ betrayed
- ❑ happy
- ❑ hurt
- ❑ lonely
- ❑ unloved
- ❑ bitter
- ❑ uninterested
- ❑ vengeful

2. How did God instruct Hosea (in Hosea 3:1) to treat his wife?

Verse to Remember

"And God is able to make all grace abound to you, so that in all things at all times, having all that you need, you will abound in every good work" (2 Corinthians 9:8).

3. What was Hosea's love and forgiveness of Gomer supposed to reflect? Of what was it symbolic?

4. Frankly, the Bible doesn't say whether Hosea's love for his wife resulted in visible protection and provision from God. But we do know that *God's standard of love provides for peace.* Consider the following excerpt from *Right From Wrong:*

> I grew up hating my father. Everyone in our small town knew about my father and his drinking. My teenage buddies made jokes about him, and I laughed, too, hoping my laughter would hide my pain. Sometimes I'd go out to the barn and find my mother lying in the manure behind the cows, beaten so badly she couldn't get up. Sometimes when he came home in a drunken stupor, I would drag him out to the barn, tie him to a stall, and leave him there to "sleep it off." As a teenager, I would tie his feet with a noose that ended around his neck, hoping he would choke himself while trying to get free. My hatred for my father was consuming; it filled my life and robbed me of peace. Not

long after becoming a Christian, though, I not only reconciled with my father, I helped him trust Christ for salvation. Fourteen months later, he died of a heart attack, but I had learned what love can do, even in the most desperate situation. Fourteen months of loving my father did much more for me than twenty years of hating him had ever done (*Right From Wrong,* 210-211).

5. *God's standard of love also provides for fulfillment.* The person who loves God and others expresses interest in the ideas and pursuits of others, often enjoys giving as much as receiving, and finds joy in sharing with others and caring for them. Such a person naturally tends to be more appreciated and successful than the self-centered individual.

6. *God's standard of love provides for spiritual blessing.* The apostle Paul described the way of love as "the most excellent way" (1 Corinthians 12:31, KJV). He knew that God prescribes a life of love for His human creations because that life results in immeasurable spiritual bounty and blessing. When we love each other, we are most like God; and when we are most like God, we experience the closest thing to paradise this side of eternity.

Today's Prayer

God, I want to "abound in every good work." I want to make right choices. I want to follow Your ways so that I might know You. Help me, today and every day, to love not in words, but in action and in truth. Amen.

Reflect

- Has your perspective on Cynthia's situation changed since you first read "The Scene on Campus" at the beginning of this unit? If so, in what way? If not, why not?

- Should we commit to God's way because of what's in it for us (His protection and provision)? Is that selfish? Is it possible for humans to respond any other way?

reflect

Review

- Write the four steps for making right choices from memory below.

C______________________________________

C______________________________________

C______________________________________

C______________________________________

review

Apply

- Are you hesitating to submit any of your relationships to God's authority? Are you dodging the 4Cs in any area of your life? If so, what will you gain by your hesitation or indecision? What might you lose?

- In which of the 4Cs are you having success?

apply

Pray

Pray "Today's Prayer" (on this page).

pray

Be a listener this week: in class, in your dorm or apartment complex, in the cafeteria. Listen closely for the different ways people use the word "love." Try to count how many times you hear the word in one day. From the study this week, and your observations of other people, has your use of the word *love* changed? Before you use the word next time, think about what you are saying.

• On a sheet of paper, list the people in your life whom you are currently finding it most difficult to love. What would it mean to commit to God's way in your relationships with them? Write by each name one loving action you can take *this week* toward that person; keep the list in your pocket or purse as a "Committing to God's Way: TO DO LIST."

• Play the "song game" described in the group Bible study (p.114) while in the car with friends, hanging out in the dorm, or waiting in line somewhere. Begin with the word "love" (you can later use other words, like "heart," or concepts, such as colors and girls' names). After the game, prompt a discussion of whether the concept of "love" in each of the songs was subjective (based only on emotion) or also objective (involving action intended to please and promote the welfare of the one being loved).

• Write a letter or note of encouragement to someone not in your circle of friends. Praise that person for something noteworthy he or she has done, or for something praiseworthy in his or her character.

• Write a letter or note of encouragement to *yourself.* Tell yourself the things of which you're most proud and for which you're most appreciative about your personality and abilities. Give yourself a "pep talk" and detail how you intend to change your treatment of yourself and others as a result of your study this week.

APPLICATION

[1] As quoted by S.I. McMillen in *None of These Diseases,* Fleming H. Revell, (Westwood, New Jersey, 1968), 78.

Notes from Session Six

Notes from Session Six
notes from session six
Notes from Session Six
notes from session six
Notes from Session Six
notes from session six
Notes from Session Six
notes from session six
notes from session six
notes from session six
notes from session six

1. I have the following questions...

2. I have the following concerns...

3. Because of this session, I feel...

It fuels billions of dollars of commerce, advertising, and industry. It sells newspapers and magazines. It dominates the talk show schedules of Oprah, Phil, Sally Jessy, Montel, Geraldo, and Gordon. It surfaces as an issue in congressional hearings and presidential primaries.

Sex.

It is vaunted and flaunted, used and abused, celebrated and debated in our culture:

> Madonna and the other mavens of MTV and the music industry unremittingly proclaim the pleasures of sex of all kinds;

Government and school officials stress the importance of "safer sex" to college students;

Parents and pastors discourage sexual involvement completely, insisting that all sexual activity should be reserved for "holy matrimony."

So what's the truth? Who do you listen to? How do you know what's right and what's wrong in the area of sex?

That question is extremely important — and urgent — among and young adults. According to George Barna, of the Barna Research Group, only twenty-three percent (23%) of the generation now entering college and approaching adulthood claim to be virgins. More than three-quarters admit to having sexual intercourse with another single person. Two out of ten single men and women (of this generation) say they have had sex with a married person, and one in fourteen married persons has had extramarital sex. Almost half (47%) of the babies born to teen and young adult females in 1992 were born to unmarried mothers.[1] And girls are having sex much earlier these days; the median age for a young woman's first act of premarital sex has fallen from 19 in 1960 to 17 in 1990. (*Right from Wrong*, 267.)

Sex Mindset
Intolerant
Ambivalent
Repressive
Permissive
Confused

"The Power of Cohorts" by Geoffrey Meredith and Charles Schewe (American Demographics, December 1994)

Moreover, our new research reveals that even students from Christian homes and good churches are crumbling under the constant pressures of a sex-crazed society. By age eighteen, more than one in four (27%) of churched young adults have experienced sexual intercourse, and over half (55%) have engaged in fondling breasts.

Such behavior is fueled (and perhaps presaged) by the fact that more than half (51%) of the young adults participating in the survey could not state that fondling of breasts was morally unacceptable. Nearly a third (30%) view the fondling of genitals as moral behavior. And one in five (18%) see sexual intercourse outside of marriage as moral. In other words, a startling percentage of Christians in this generation think that heavy petting — even sexual intercourse — between two unmarried individuals is perfectly moral (especially, the survey reveals, if the participants are "in love"). (*Right from Wrong,* 273.)

Simply put, a large number of today's college students — even Christians — are sexually active, and many of them believe there's nothing wrong with their activity. . .at least not in their situations.

The question is: are they right?

Few things offend young adults aged 18 to 34. Among young men, 61 percent claim they seldom if ever take offense at sex in advertising. Young women are the most common lure in sexy ads, but 44 percent of them aren't bothered by the association. Just 15 percent of young men and 24 percent of young women frequently or always find sexual references offensive. An additional 24 percent of young men and 32 percent of young women admit that they offended occasionally.

"Safe Sex in Advertising," by Doris Walsh (American Demographics, April 1994)

CASE STUDY

Cynthia glanced at her watch as the judge sentenced her roommate, Teri, to 80 hours of community service. Teri was still mad at her, and Cynthia admitted to herself that she was still mad herself at the way Teri had been treating her lately. But she had swallowed her anger and not only relayed Rosemarie's message about the change of court date, but had also sat beside Teri all morning while waiting for her case to be called, explaining that she did it so Teri "wouldn't have to go through it alone."

She went straight from the courthouse to her afternoon classes, skipping lunch, and returned to the dorm just in time to gather her Bible and notebook and head for her campus Bible study. As she turned to head out the open door, she stopped abruptly when she noticed that Rosemarie filled the doorway.

"Hi," Cynthia said. A silent moment passed between them, and they faced each other awkwardly.

"Is this a bad time?" Rosemarie asked. Tears ringed her eyes. "You're about to go somewhere, aren't you?"

Cynthia suppressed the urge to look at her watch. She shook her head. "This isn't a bad time," she said. "Come on in." She pulled Rosemarie into the room by her wrist and shut the door behind her.

"I just —" Rosemarie began, sitting in the molded plastic chair beside Cynthia's bed. She swallowed. "Teri told me what you did this morning."

Cynthia shrugged. She dropped her Bible and notebook onto the bed and sat, folding one leg beneath her while the other dangled over the edge of the bed.

"I just needed to talk to somebody," Rosemarie said, and fell silent again.

"What's wrong, Rosemarie?"

Rosemarie explained, through much tearful starting and stopping, that she had gone to a clinic last night for a pregnancy test. The pregnancy test had been negative, but the blood test they gave her had revealed something else.

Cynthia held her breath, fearing the worst.

"I have something called chlamydia," Rosemarie said.

"What's that? Is it serious?"

Rosemarie shrugged. "I have to take medication. The nurse said I could resume 'normal sexual relations' in a couple weeks. Cynthia," she cried, a tear streaming down each cheek, "I don't want to 'resume normal sexual relations'."

Cynthia opened her mouth to speak, then closed it. She crouched in front of Rosemarie and wrapped her arms around her. The two girls cried together in silence for a few moments, until Rosemarie lifted her head from Cynthia's shoulder.

"Jonathan won't understand," she continued. "He says there's nothing wrong with what we've been doing. He says it's just an expression of our love for each other, but —" She stopped, and her voice suddenly became smaller. "But I feel wrong every time we do it, and I feel sad and. . . and disappointed when it's over."

"Have you told Jonathan how you feel?"

Rosemarie nodded. "He just says I must not love him if I don't want to give myself to him."

"Do you love him?"

She nodded again. "That's what makes it so impossible."

Cynthia sighed. She opened her mouth again to speak, but she closed it again. She didn't know what to say.

CASE STUDY

Questions

1. First, what do you think about Cynthia going to court with Teri? Do you think she made a good decision? Would you have acted differently?

According to the report, 22% of women say they have been forced to do sexual thing they didn't want to, usually by someone they loved. But only 3% of men admit to ever forcing themselves on women.
"Now for the Truth About Americans and Sex," by Philip Elmer-Dewitt (Time 10/17/94)

2. How do you respond to Rosemarie's problem? How do you respond to her boyfriend's reasoning?

3. What would you do if you were in Cynthia's place in the scene above? What would you do if you were in Rosemarie's place?

BIBLE STUDY PASSAGE

ave you ever used any of the following items?

- voltage meter
- turkey baster
- seam ripper
- plunger ("plumber's helper")
- leather punch
- car jack
- chopsticks
- rototiller

How many of the items do you think you could *identify* by sight? Each of those objects on the list is a tool, utensil, or machine with a fairly specialized use. It wouldn't do much good, for example, to try to till your garden with a plunger or eat fried rice with a plumber's helper.

Just as the voltage meter and car jack were created with a certain purpose in mind, so sex was created to be used in a specific way.

Genesis 2:4-25

This is the account of the heavens and the earth when they were created.

When the LORD God made the earth and the heavens — and no shrub of the field had yet appeared on the earth and no plant of the field had yet sprung up, for the LORD God had not sent rain on the earth and there was no man to work the ground, but streams came up from the earth and watered the whole surface of the ground — the LORD God formed the man from the dust of the ground and breathed into his nostrils the breath of life, and the man became a living being.

Now the LORD God had planted a garden in the east, in Eden; and there he put the man he had formed. And the LORD God made all kinds of trees grow out of the ground — trees that were pleasing to the eye and good for food. In the middle of the garden were the tree of life and the tree of the knowledge of good and evil.

A river watering the garden flowed from Eden; from there it was separated into four headwaters. The name of the first is the Pishon; it winds through the entire land of Havilah, where there is gold. (The gold of that land is good; aromatic resin and onyx are also there.) The name of the second river is the Gihon; it winds through the entire land of Cush. The name of the third river is the Tigris; it runs along the east side of Asshur. And the fourth river is the Euphrates.

The LORD God took the man and put him in the Garden of Eden to work it and take care of it. And the LORD God commanded the man, "You are free to eat from any tree in the garden; but you must not eat from the tree of the knowledge of good and evil, for when you eat of it you will surely die."

The LORD God said, "It is not good for the man to be alone. I will make a helper suitable for him."

Now the LORD God had formed out of the ground all the beasts of the field and all the birds of the air. He brought them to the man to see what he would name them; and whatever the man called each living creature, that was its name. So the man gave names to all the livestock, the birds of the air and all the beasts of the field.

But for Adam no suitable helper was found. So the LORD God caused the man to fall into a deep sleep; and while he was sleeping, he took one of the man's ribs and closed up the place with flesh. Then the LORD God made a woman from the rib he had taken out of the man, and he brought her to the man.

The man said, "This is now bone of my bones and flesh of my flesh; she shall be called 'woman,' for she was taken out of man." For this reason a man will leave his father and mother and be united to his wife, and they will become one flesh.

The man and his wife were both naked, and they felt no shame.

Read

Carefully read Genesis 2:4-25.

Discuss

1. According to the above verses, who created the concept of "male" and "female?" Does that fact have any significance? Discuss.

2. The text is not explicit, but who do you think it implies as the author of sex? (See also Genesis 1:28.) Does that realization have any significance? Discuss.

3. Do you think human sexuality was among the characteristics of God's creation that He pronounced "very good" in Genesis 1:31?

❑ Yes ❑ No

4. According to the above passage, which of the following *characteristics* did God's design for sex include? (check all that

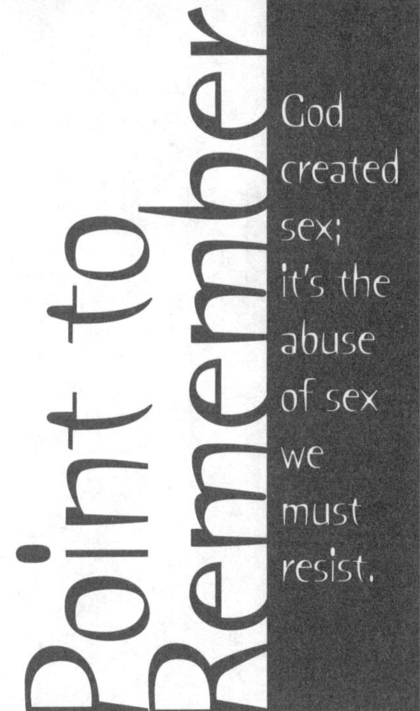

apply and discuss how you arrived at your answer)

- ❑ between a man and a woman
- ❑ an exclusive relationship
- ❑ between a husband and wife
- ❑ a lifelong relationship
- ❑ free of shame and guilt
- ❑ other?

5. According to Genesis 1:28 and 31, which of the following *purposes* did God design sex to accomplish? Check all that apply and discuss how you arrived at your answer.

- ❑ procreation
- ❑ unity
- ❑ true emotional intimacy
- ❑ other?

Reflect

• How many of the above characteristics and purposes are stressed or even mentioned in our sex-crazed culture? Consider movies, television, magazines, advertisements, government policy, etc. What things does the culture emphasize?

• Do you think God created sex as a concession to human sinfulness? Why or why not?

• Do you think God intended sex to be as powerful and pleasurable as it is today? Why or why not?

• What is the difference between a sex drive and a sex life? Is either one OK for unmarried persons?

• What can happen when sex is used in a way other than that for which God designed it?

• What light if any does this study throw on Rosemarie's problem?

Apply

• Consider how *you* view sex. Is your view of sex based on God's design or the cultural concept?

• To what degree do you think your hormones dictate your sexual behavior? Your emotions? Your spiritual convictions? Your understanding of God's Word?

• Is there any part of your thought life or behavior that you need to align with God's design? How can you begin today to do that? If you're not sure, seek advice from a trusted friend or mentor.

Pray

Pray "Today's Prayer" (on this page).

Today's Prayer

(Read aloud) Creator God, if there is any topic on which our world needs Your guidance, it is sex. Give us the wisdom to see through the lies that abound in our culture. Give us the strength to live out our sexuality the way You intended, in Jesus' name, Amen.

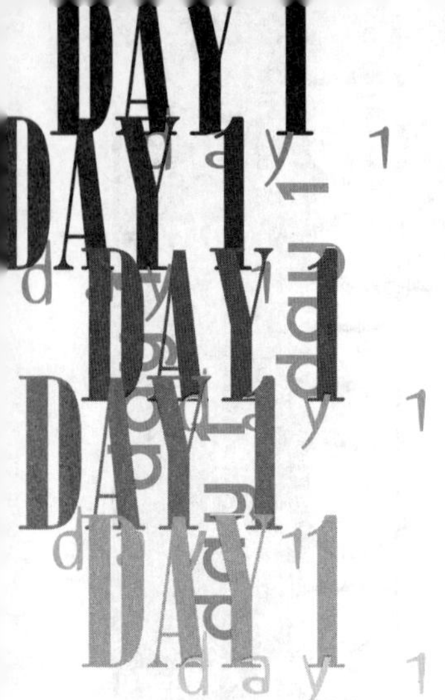

One in five (18%) of churched young adults say they think sexual intercourse between unmarried persons is morally acceptable; more than twice that number (46%) said that they would be more likely to have sex with someone if they "were in love with the person."

Forty-four percent (44%) say that they would be more likely to have sex with a person they "really intended to marry."

One in four (26%) say they would be more likely to have sex if they were positive a pregnancy would not result. An identical number responded that they would be more likely to "go all the way" if they could know that their parents would not find out, and one in five (22%) said they would be more likely to have sex if they felt that their parents "would not mind." One in nine (11%) said that being "strongly encouraged" by friends to have sex would make them more likely to do so.

Think Thru

1. Which of the above stated factors do you think affects the rightness or wrongness of sexual activity? (check all that apply)
   - ❑ if the couple are in love
   - ❑ if the couple intend to marry
   - ❑ if the couple are sure a pregnancy will not result
   - ❑ if the couple know their parents will not find out
   - ❑ if the couple are confident their parents would not mind
   - ❑ if the couple are strongly encouraged by friends to have sex

2. Rosemarie (in "The Scene on Campus") has been sexually involved with her boyfriend for some time, yet she told Cynthia she wasn't comfortable with their behavior. Why do you think she has become intimate with Jonathan? List the things below that you think prompted her decision to become physically involved.

Verse to Remember

"It is God's will that you should be sanctified; that you should avoid sexual immorality" (1 Thessalonians 4:3).

3. Do you think Rosemarie expects to enjoy some immediate benefits as a result of her decision? What would such benefits be?

4. Do those benefits make her behavior *right?*
   - ❑ Yes, because
   - ❑ No, because

think thru

You see, Rosemarie and her boyfriend, Jonathan, are trying to judge right and wrong (which is objective) by their *passions* (which are subjective). They are letting their raging hormones cloud their judgment of right and wrong. What *should* they do rather than justifying their actions and proclaiming them "right" because of their plans and passions?

C____________________ the C________________________

If they were to **consider the choice,** however, they would remember that their choice is not between what *they* think is right or wrong, but between what is right or wrong, regardless of what they think.

Read

1. Second Samuel 11 contains the story of David, and a horribly wrong choice he made. Read 2 Samuel 11:1-17,26-27.

Study

1. Do you think David's choice was right or wrong? (circle one) Why?

2. Do you think David might have tried to justify his choice to become physically involved with Bathsheba? What kinds of reasons could he have given to make his conduct seem "right"?

3. Do you think David tried to judge right and wrong (which is objective) by his passions (which were subjective)?

❑ Yes ❑ No

4. Does the Scriptural account give any indication that David considered the choice?

❑ Yes ❑ No

5. Do you think he considered the choice (at that moment) as a choice between what was objectively right and what was objectively wrong — regardless of what he thought or felt?

❑ Yes ❑ No

Apply

• What about you? Do you ever try to judge right and wrong by your passions?

❑ Yes ❑ No

• If your answer was yes, in what situations are you most likely to try to judge right and wrong by your passions?

• What can you do today to **consider the choice,** to start making your choices based on a belief in an objective, universal, constant standard of right and wrong?

Pray

Spend a few moments in prayer, perhaps using the following as a guideline:

• Praise God because He is righteous, loving, holy, and true.
• Talk to God honestly about the changes you would like to make in the way you make choices, and the changes you would like to see in the way the youth in your life make choices.
• Ask Him to give you patience and perseverance as you continue in this study.
• Pray for your family and friends, asking God to use you to bless them.
• Conclude with "Today's Prayer" (on this page).

Today's Prayer

Father, once again I submit to You and to Your revelation. Remind me through today's study that You are the Standard of all that is righteous and holy, in Jesus' name, Amen.

In December 1962, a London engineer stopped his train in the midst of a lingering fog, a fog that was thick even by London standards. Concluding perhaps that the fog was too thick and his vision too impaired to proceed any farther, the experienced train man opened the door and stepped down from his cab into 40 feet of water. He had no idea that he had stopped the train on a bridge. The engineer was one of more than 100 Londoners who died that week from fog.

That is not the only tragedy caused by fog, of course; nor does tragedy result only from changes in atmosphere. Another kind of fog often endangers people who must decide between right and wrong in matters pertaining to love and sex. Students in love — regardless of their age — often seem to be enveloped in a kind of fog that blurs their sight and clouds their perception of right and wrong. If they are not equipped with strong biblical values, they are likely to make disastrous choices in the area of love and sex.

In "The Scene on Campus," Rosemarie is not **considering the choice** as a choice between what is right or wrong objectively (regardless of what *she* thinks). Consequently, she's not proceeding to the next step in the 4Cs process. What *would* Rosemarie discover if she were to **compare her action to God?** What would she learn by tracing her action through precept and principle to the Person of God Himself?

Study

1. *Precept*

• In biblical terms, sexual immorality is all extramarital, including premarital, sex. God has spoken through the law, and He has made His standard clear: all sexual involvement outside of marriage is wrong. Look up the following precepts in your Bible, and match the first phrase of each precept to the second by drawing a line to connect them.

1. You are to abstain from food sacrificed to idols, from blood, from the meat of strangled animals and from sexual immorality.	All other sins a man commits are outside his body, but he who sins sexually sins against his own body (1Corinthians 6:18).
2. It is God's will that you should be sanctified:	because these are improper for God's holy people (Ephesians. 5:3).
3. Flee from sexual immorality.	You will do well to avoid these things. (Acts 15:29).
4. Put to death, therefore, whatever belongs to your earthly nature:	that you should avoid sexual immorality (1Thessalonians 4:3).
5. We should not commit sexual immorality, as some of them did—	sexual immorality, impurity, lust, evil desires and greed, which is idolatry (Colossians 3:5).
6. But among you there must not be even a hint of sexual immorality, or of any kind of impurity, or of greed,	And in one day twenty-three thousand of them died (1 Corinthians 10:8).

2. ***Principle***

• What positive principle or principles do you think lie behind those precepts?

• The biblical commands to "flee sexual immorality" are based on God's standards for sex, which actually incorporate three principles: love, purity, and faithfulness.

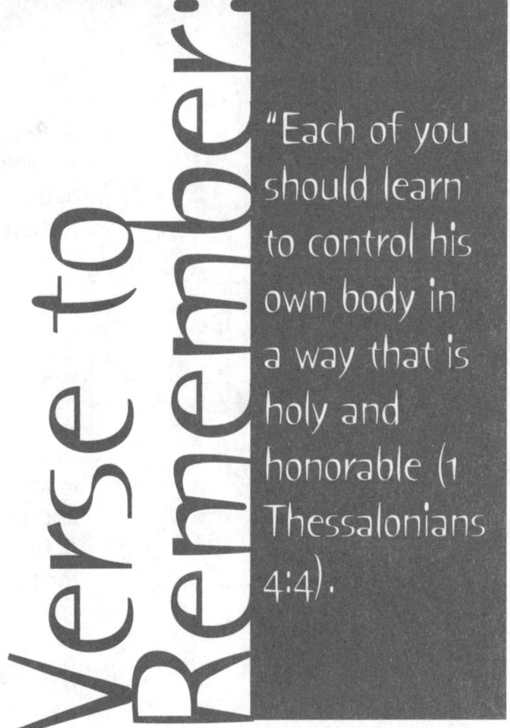

A. According to the Bible (Romans 13:9-10 and Ephesians 5:28), true love is evident when the happiness, health, and spiritual growth of another person is as important to you as your own.

B. God's standard for sex is one of **purity.** Copy Hebrews 13:4 below.

He designed sex to be enjoyed in a husband-wife relationship, for procreation (Genesis 1:28), for spiritual unity (Genesis 2:24), and for recreation (Proverbs 5:18, 19). It's meant to form an unbroken circle, a pure union: two virgins entering an exclusive relationship. That circle, that union, can be *broken* even before marriage, if one or both of the partners has not kept the marriage bed pure by waiting to have sex until it can be done in the purity of a husband-wife relationship.

C. God's standard for sex is also one of **faithfulness**. Love "always protects, always trusts, always hopes, always perseveres" (1 Corinthians 13:7). "Love and faithfulness meet together" (Psalm 85:10). In practical terms, this means that true love requires a commitment of two people to remain faithful to each other. That is why marriage is central to biblical sexuality, because it binds two people together in a lifelong commitment. If love is to produce the emotional, physical, and spiritual intimacy it is designed to produce, it must be committed, faithful love. Two students may be talking about marriage, they might even get engaged, *but until they are husband and wife, they have not fully committed to each other and fulfilled God's requirement for sex.*

God's precepts regarding human sexuality are grounded upon the principles of love, purity, and faithfulness. Those principles, in turn, reflect the person of God Himself.

3. ***Person***

• Those principles are right because they are from God — they reflect his nature and character. Read the following Bible verses and complete the statement that follows each verse.

1 John 4:8 God is ______________________________

1 John 3:3 He (God) is__________________________

Deuteronomy. 7:9 He (God) is the ______________ God.

Rosemarie and Jonathan need to compare their sexual activity to the nature and character of God (instead of justifying it by their passions. Help them determine whether the following statements are true or false by circling T for true and F for false.

T F Our action is loving; it promotes the happiness, health, and spiritual growth of the other person

T F Our action is pure; it does not defile the marriage bed by permitting activity that should be reserved for a husband or wife

T F Our action is faithful; both partners have made a lifetime commitment of marriage

reflect

Reflect

• Because God is pure, sexual impurity is an offense against Him. Because He is faithful, sex outside of a marriage commitment is an affront to Him. King David, who sinned with Bathsheba, later repented; he confessed to God, "Against you, you only, have I sinned and done what is evil in your sight" (Psalm 51:4). Was David ignoring the fact that his sin had affected other people, resulting in the death of Bathsheba's husband, Uriah, and of the baby Bathsheba bore David? No, he was acknowledging the fundamental fact that when he sinned with Bathsheba, he sinned against the Lawgiver. His act was wrong because it offended God's standard for sex: love, purity, and faithfulness.

apply

Apply

• Do your relationships conform to that standard?

• Is your romantic and sexual activity based on an objective, constant, and universal standard? Or are you tolerating wrong attitudes or actions in this area?

• If your actions conform to God's standard in this area, read Psalm 91:1-4, praising God and placing your trust in His strength.

• If your actions do not conform to God's standard in this area, turn to David's prayer in Psalm 51, and read verses 1-12, making them your prayer.

Pray

Close your study time today by asking God to make your relationships (present and/or future) loving, faithful, and pure relationships that honor Him and your mate.

Today's Prayer

Father, thank You for making me a sexual being. Thank You for sexual desires, and for the unity they create between a husband and wife. Please teach me to control my body in a way that is holy and honorable, in the mighty name of Jesus, Amen.

True Love Waits is an international campaign designed to challenge teenagers and college students to remain sexually pure until marriage. To date, hundreds of thousands of young people have signed covenant cards which state: "Believing that true love waits, I make a commitment to God, myself, my family, my friends, my future mate, and my future children to be sexually abstinent from this day until the day I enter a biblical marriage relationship." More that 210,000 covenant cards were displayed on the National Mall in Washington, D.C., on July 29, 1994, as part of the True Love Waits National Celebration, Approximately 25,000 young people attended the event.

Rosemarie is in trouble. She has been uncomfortable with her sexual involvement, but she's not sure why; and she doesn't know why Jonathan's claim that it's OK rings so hollow. She may be trying to ignore what her heart and mind know: that she should turn from her own selfish ways and commit to God's way.

Rosemarie and Jonathan are not the first to make that mistake (chances are, you've done the same thing yourself...if not in the area of sexual involvement, perhaps in some other area).

Remember King David and his incredibly bad choices with Bathsheba? You already know that the story didn't end after David engineered the death of Uriah, Bathsheba's husband.

> Rather than peaceable kingdoms, many of today's campuses have turned into depressing incubators of economic, academic and psychological tensions where the demand for therapy is rising even faster than tuition.
>
> *"America's Best Colleges," by Mel Elfin with Andrea R. Wright (U.S. News & World Report, 9/26/94)*

Read

Read 2 Samuel 12:1-13.

Study

1. How did David finally come to admit the wrongness of his actions?

2. Do you think verse 13 reflects
   - a sudden realization or,
   - David sensed his sinfulness all along?

   (circle one)

   Why did you answer as you did?

Verse to Remember

"Create in me a pure heart, O God, and renew a right spirit within me" (Psalm 51:10).

3. Do you think verse 13 corresponds with any of the 4Cs? If so, which one?

4. Read Psalm 51:1-17, the song David composed after the prophet Nathan confronted him with his sin. Based on these verses, do you think David committed to God's way?

   ❑ Yes ❑ No

   Why or why not?

5. How is David's situation similar to Rosemarie's and Jonathan's?

6. How is it different?

7. What do you think committing to God's way would involve for Rosemarie? (check all that apply)

- ❑ break up with Jonathan
- ❑ keep her mouth shut and see what happens
- ❑ admit her sexual sin to God
- ❑ marry Jonathan immediately
- ❑ join the circus
- ❑ determine from now on to save all forms of sexual intimacy for marriage
- ❑ resolve to start anew to build a relationship that reflects love, purity, and faithfulness
- ❑ become a nun
- ❑ focus on the spiritual, emotional, and intellectual parts of their relationship while steering away from physical intimacy
- ❑ avoid being alone with Jonathan in dark or secluded places
- ❑ avoid being alone with anybody in dark or secluded places
- ❑ avoid dark or secluded places

Reflect

reflect

- Do you think committing to God's way would be easy for Rosemarie?

- What do you think would be hardest for her?

Apply

apply

- What is hardest for you about committing to God's way in this area?

- How can you give that problem to God?

Today's Prayer

Sovereign Lord, I have given my heart, my mind, and my soul to You. I give You my sexuality, too. Help me daily to turn from my own ways, and commit to You in this area as in all others. For I ask it in the name of Jesus, who gave Himself for me, Amen.

Pray

pray

Close today's study by writing your own "Psalm 51" below in which you admit God's sovereignty, submit to His version of what's right or wrong, and commit to following His ways in the power of His Holy Spirit.

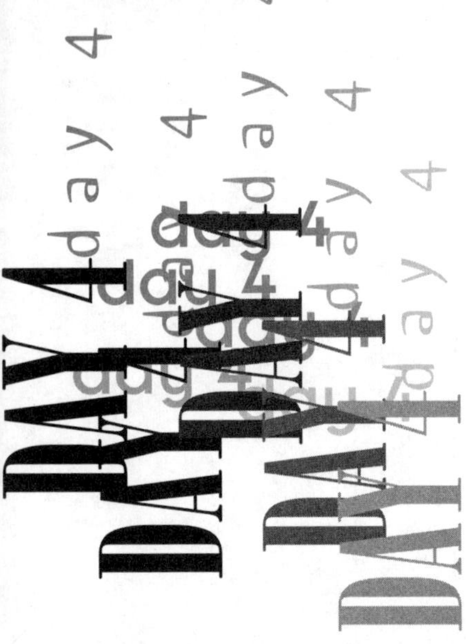

Like all of His precepts, God's standards of sexual abstinence before marriage and faithfulness within marriage are meant to protect us and provide for us.

Rosemarie and Jonathan have short-circuited God's loving plans for them, and the results (her pregnancy scare and contraction of a serious sexually transmitted disease, to name just two examples) are tragic.

But while she can't erase the consequences of her action, she can still, if she considers the choice, compares it to God, and commits to God's way, enjoy the future benefits of right choices as she learns to count on God's protection and provision.

Q. My girlfriend and I have been together for three years and four months. We would like to get married someday, and are willing to be patient and make sure it's God's will. We agree that sex should be kept within marriage. But that's our problem: the desire for sex. We both thank God for that desire, but a lot of times we've come close to having sex. We've done a lot of heavy petting, and believe me, the temptation to go all the way is there. What are some alternatives we could use to get out of that "late night, on the couch" rut? We really don't want sex to break us up, we just want some advice!

"Love, Sex & the Whole Person: Living with Unfulfilled Desires," by Tim Stafford (Campus Life, September 1992)

Read

Turn again to 2 Samuel 11:26-12:25.

Study

The story of David and Bathsheba graphically depicts the results of David's refusal to follow God's way. Based on the above account in 2 Samuel, answer the following multiple choice questions (circle the correct choice):

1. As a result of David's choice, Bathsheba became:
   a) pregnant
   b) David's wife
   c) a widow
   d) all of the above
2. As a result of David's choice, God:
   a) stopped loving David
   b) rewarded David
   c) was displeased with David
   d) struck David with leprosy
3. As a result of David's choice, the baby:
   a) grew up to be king
   b) became a great warrior
   c) brought years of joy to his parents
   d) none of the above
4. As a result of David's choice, David:
   a) brought shame on the name of the Lord
   b) lost his firstborn son
   c) spent seven days in agony and uncertainty
   d) all of the above

(Answers: 1.(d), 2. (c), 3. (d), 4. (d)

David's story illustrates the fact that adherence to God's standards in this (as in every) area protects from many undesirable and devastating consequences.

1. *God's standards for sexual behavior protect from guilt.* Because God defines right and wrong, when we transgress his standards, we will invariably suffer guilt. Rosemarie confessed to Cynthia, "I feel wrong every time we do it, and I feel sad and. . . and disappointed when it's over." Jonathan's repeated assertions that he and Rosemarie had no reason to feel guilty were not sufficient to erase the guilt on her heart; they felt it necessary to convince themselves because they did feel guilty. . .as will anyone who does wrong.

2. *God's standards for sexual behavior protect from unplanned pregnancies and abortions.* Every day in America, 2,795 teenage girls get pregnant and 1,106 have an abortion. Those girls who carry their babies for the full term often face overwhelming difficulties; many drop out of school, many experience physical problems, many feel left out of "normal" teen activities because of their responsibility to a child. Those girls who abort their children are not delivered from such consequences; abortion produces traumatic results, too. Over half report preoccupation with the aborted child, flashbacks of the abortion experience, and nightmares related to the abortion.[2]

3. *God's standards for sexual behavior protect from sexually transmitted diseases.* Every day in America, 4,219 young adults contract a sexually transmitted disease, some of which are deadly, many of which have horrifying consequences. Yet not one of those incidents has occurred between two mutually faithful partners who entered the relationship sexually pure. . . because God's standards for sexual behavior protect from sexually transmitted diseases.

4. *God's standards for sexual behavior protect from emotional distress.* The emotional costs of sexual immorality are immeasurable. One young adult explained the effects of her sexual involvement in these words:

> *"...Having premarital sex was the most horrifying experience of my life. It wasn't at all the emotionally satisfying experience the world deceived me into believing. I felt as if my insides were being exposed and my heart left unattended...I know God has forgiven me of this haunting sin, but I also know I can never have my virginity back. I dread the day that I have to tell the man I truly love and wish to marry that he is not the only one, though I wish he were."*

Those who heed God's standard are protected from the consequences sexual immorality (whether premarital or extramarital) breeds: suspicion, disappointment, sorrow, stress, emptiness, and many other destructive emotions.

"I am the LORD your God, who teaches you what is best for you, who directs you in the way you should go" (Isaiah 48:17).

Reflect

• Can you think of any other ways in which committing to God's standard in the area of sex might protect you?

• It seems extremely difficult for some people to wait until marriage to have sex. Do you think engaging in sexual behavior short of intercourse (such as petting) makes it easier or harder to wait?

Apply

• Has the "fog" that so often surrounds sexual decisions cleared for you as a result of this study? Why or why not?

• Are you admitting God's sovereignty, submitting to His authority, and committing to His ways? If not, in which area are you having the most trouble? Is there a respected Christian whose counsel you can seek in overcoming that difficulty?

Pray

• Spend a few moments meditating on the "Verse to Remember" (on this page) and then pray "Today's Prayer."

Today's Prayer

My Lord and my God, thank You for teaching me what is best for me and for leading me in the way I should go. Reinforce in my mind the conviction that Your commandments about sex are not meant to limit my enjoyment but to enhance it, and to protect me from the emotional, physical, and spiritual dangers that result from abusing Your precious gift. Amen.

Sex is right when it reflects the nature and character of God Himself, who is loving, pure, and faithful. The "evidence of truth" (that is, the evidence of God's loving motivation) reveals that sex as God designed it is also beneficial.

Think Thru

Circle the following statements T for "true" or F for "false".

T F God isn't crazy about sex
T F The Bible doesn't mention sex
T F Christians shouldn't think about sex
T F Sex came into the world as a result of sin
T F God has left His people free to experiment with sex how ever they wish
T F The Bible always depicts sex as dirty
T F Sex was God's idea
T F God understands sex better than anyone else
T F God wants men and women to get the most out of sex

(Answers: The first six statements are false; the latter three are true.)

Understand

The Song of Solomon is an ancient love poem written as a dialogue between a man and his wife. The language is highly figurative. It depicts the joy of love and sex within marriage.

Read

Read Song of Solomon 4:1-11, in which Solomon extols his wife's beauty and sexuality.

Verse to Remember

"To Him who is able to keep you from falling and to present you before his glorious presence without fault and with great joy — to the only God our Savior be glory, majesty, power and authority, through Jesus Christ our Lord, before all ages, now and forevermore! Amen (Jude 24-25).

Reflect

- Does anything about the Song of Solomon surprise you? If so, what?

- Do you think such straightforward language about sex is inappropriate for the Bible? Why or why not?

Study

In what ways do God's standards in the area of sex provide for us?

1. *God's standard for sexual behavior provides for spiritual rewards.* The blessing of a clear conscience and an unhindered walk with God are inestimable. It is an immeasurable blessing to be able to stand before an altar and proclaim the singular devotion of your body to your mate and to God. The sexual relationship between a husband and wife is not only pleasurable, it is sacred.

2. *God's standard for sexual behavior provides for peace of mind.* Two people who adhere to God's wise model will enjoy a relationship free of fear, free of disease, free of the "ghosts" of past partners, and free of "emotional baggage" as a result of a past immoral relationship.

3. *God's standard for sexual behavior provides for trust.* Sexual purity and faithfulness before marriage contributes to an atmosphere of trust within marriage. That trust provides peace of mind for both partners when they are apart; each knows that the other is worthy of trust. Why? Because, in the period before their marriage, they proved their character, their maturity, and their self-control.

4. *God's standard for sexual behavior provides for true intimacy.* God's standard for sexual behavior produces a degree of intimacy that only exists in the committed exclusivity of a marriage relationship. "For this reason," God said, "a man will leave his father and mother and be united to his wife, and they will become one flesh" (Genesis 2:24).

5. *God's design for sexual intimacy protects from many dangers.* It provides the best climate for the enjoyment of spiritual rewards, peace of mind, trust, intimacy, and many other benefits, to be enjoyed in a life-long relationship of purity and faithfulness.

Today's Prayer

God, I know You are able to keep me from falling in this area as in others. Through Your Holy Spirit, make me wise in avoiding temptation, strong in resisting temptation, and victorious in conquering temptation, through Jesus Christ I pray, Amen.

Review

- Write the four steps for making right choices from memory below.

C________________________________

C________________________________

C________________________________

C________________________________

Apply

- Do you think the evidence of truth (the ways in which God's standards protect us and provide for us) is compelling enough to affect your behavior? If so, in what way? If not, why not?

- Have you begun implementing the 4Cs into your decision-making processes? If so, what effect do you think it's had? If not, why haven't you begun yet? Is your hesitation due to rebellion, unwillingness, a lack of understanding, or something else?

- If God is "able to keep you from falling and to present you before his glorious presence without fault" (Jude 24), do you think His Holy Spirit can give you the strength to obey Him in this area as in others? Ask Him to do that.

Pray

Pray "Today's Prayer" (on this page).

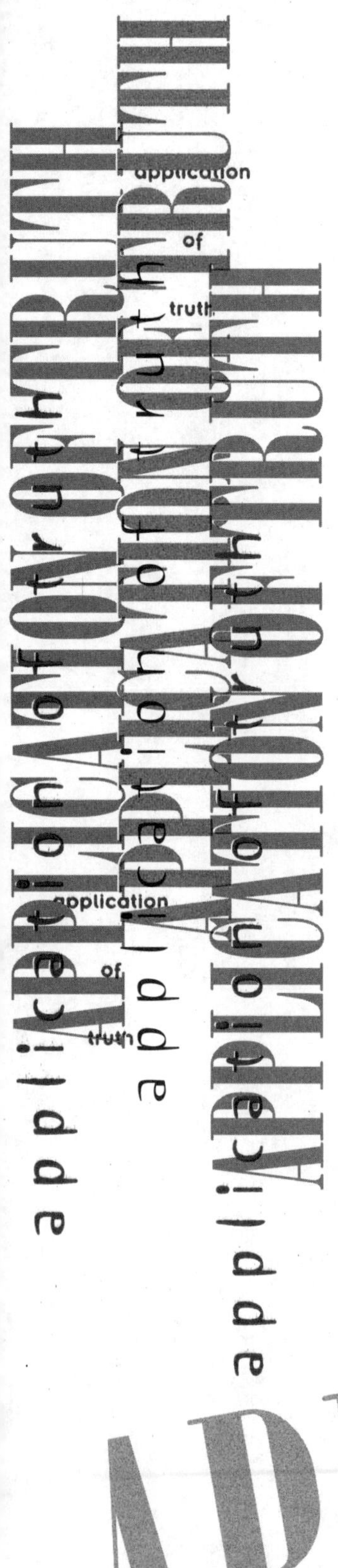

Write a letter to God, thanking Him for the gift of sex and confiding to Him what you want your sex life to be like with your mate or future mate. Seal the letter in an envelope, and keep it tucked in your Bible at the Song of Solomon. You may even choose someday to present it to your new wife or husband on your wedding night!

• Learn to evaluate prime-time television shows and how they deal with love and sexual relations. Get together with a small group of friends and discuss if what you see on the screen depicts a biblical standard of sexual intimacy.

• Spend some time thinking about your personal relationship with God through His Son Jesus Christ, and what He has brought you through as a result of this study. Write down what God has been doing in your life lately. What have you been learning about yourself and the nature of God? That is called a "testimony." A testimony involves your life before you had a personal relationship with God, what change happened when you accepted Christ, and most importantly what God is doing with your life right now! Write out your testimony on a sheet of paper. It should be brief, no more than three paragraphs. Find a friend who will help you to practice sharing that testimony, so that you will be prepared, if the opportunity arises, to share the truth about the moral maze with someone else.

• Is Scripture memory a regular part of your time spent growing as a Christian? If you do not yet have a Scripture memory program, take three-by-five inch cards and cut them in half. Print a short verse of Scripture on the card. Carry these cards with you in your pocket, purse, backpack, or wallet; tape them to your mirror in your bathroom; anything you can do to see them on a regular basis is helpful. Try to memorize at least one verse each week. God will use those verses as gentle reminders of His truth to you each day. John 10:10 is a good verse to begin with, as are the "Verse to Remember" at the beginning of each day's study in this book.

• If you have an artistic bent, make a statement (and provoke interesting conversations!) by covering your Bible with a brown paper bag. Label it, "Sex Without Guilt: A Handbook." Or use a similar idea of your own devising.

APPLICATION

[1] Figures as cited by George Barna, *Baby Busters: The Disillusioned Generation,* (Chicago: Northfield Publishing, 1994), pp.122-123.

[2] Anne Catherine Speckhard, "Psycho-Social Aspects of Stress Following Abortion" (doctoral dissertation, University of Minnesota, 1985), n.p.

Notes from Session Seven

Notes from Session Seven
Notes from Session Seven
Notes from Session Seven
Notes from Session Seven
notes from session seven
notes from session seven
notes from session seven
notes from session seven
notes from session seven
notes from session seven
notes from session seven

1. I have the following questions...

2. I have the following concerns...

3. Because of this session, I feel...

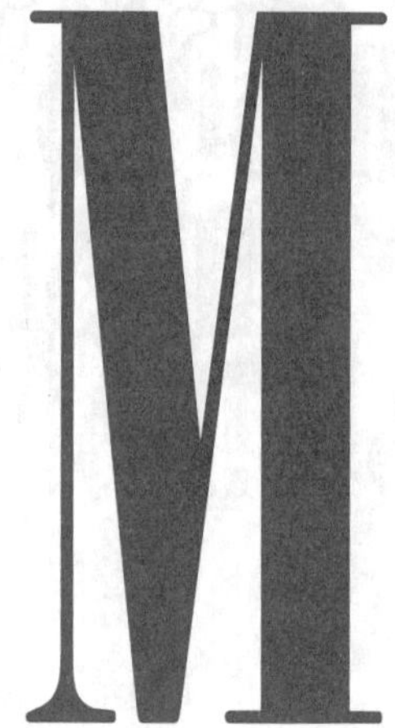

Many years ago, a young prince watched as his nation was conquered by a foreign army. The foreigners took him prisoner and carted him hundreds of miles away to a strange city, where he was ordered to be trained for the king's service. The prince was required to learn the language and literature of the conquering nation, and was served daily helpings of sumptuous food and wine.

However, the prince was a Jew, which meant that he observed strict rules about what he could eat, and how his food had to be prepared. He explained his predicament to his superior.

"I'd like to help you," the official said, "but it's my job to keep you strong and healthy; the king will have my head — literally — if you become weak or pale."

So the prince proposed a solution for him and the other Jews who were training for the king's service. "Do this," he said. "Give me and my buddies nothing but vegetables to eat and water to drink for ten days. Then compare our appearance with that of the young men who eat the royal food. If we don't look as healthy as they do, you can do whatever you want with us."

At the end of the trial period, the young prince and his friends looked healthier and better nourished than the men who feasted on ham and eggs. The prince and his friends not only stood firm for their convictions; they also quickly became the king's most valued advisors.

That young prince's name was Daniel, and his story is found in the Old Testament book that bears his name. He was a trusted advisor of several kings, and his whole life seems to have been a series of challenges in which he stood for truth in the face of great and dangerous opposition (which once included a den of lions, of course).

Daniel took a stand for truth regardless of the cost. He determined to do the right thing because he was convinced that God's commands (which proceed from his nature) were true. He may also have been aware that right choices would, in the long run, bring the greatest benefits.

You see, it's not only important to *discern* what is right; you must also do it. And standing for truth is not like pledging a fraternity or passing your GRE; you don't just do it once and forget about it. Standing for truth is a lifestyle. It's a whole new way of living and thinking and choosing. It's a day-by-day, minute-by-minute decision to accept the truth — as it's revealed in God's precepts, principles, and Person — and to submit to His leadership, to His control.

That may seem pretty overwhelming, of course. After all, who follows the truth every day? Who does the right thing every minute? Nobody's perfect — except for Jesus, and He's the key to standing for truth. Remember, He said, "I am the way and the truth and the life" (John 14:6). The truth is alive! If you have trusted Jesus Christ as Savior and Lord, you have the Truth living inside you. So, you see, standing for truth isn't about rules; it's about relationship... a personal relationship with (and constant dependence on) the Truth Himself!

I challenge you to never again think of the commands of God as "dos and don'ts," "shall and shall nots." See them as God's way to reveal His very nature and character to you. See them as the expression of God's loving desire to protect you and provide for you. Take a stand for truth, let the Truth live in you and through you, and share the Truth with others.

Cynthia turned excitedly to Rosemarie as she pulled a candy bar out of the vending machine in the Student Union building.

"Oh, I almost forgot to tell you." Her eyes sparkled like a tiny fireworks display. "You remember Jesse, my friend from back home?" Rosemarie nodded. "He's a computer science major. Anyway, he finally said he's going to start going to Bible study with us!"

Of all powers, love is the most powerful and the most powerless. It is the most powerful because it alone can conquer that final and most impregnable stronghold which is the human heart. It is the most powerless because it can do nothing except by consent.
disciplines for the inner life, by Bob Benson, Sr. and Michael W. Benson, Generoux/Nelson, Nashville, © 1989.

"That's great," Rosemarie answered.

"He had a tougher first semester than I did, in a lot of ways," Cynthia said. She spoke rapidly, excitedly. "He started *really* questioning his faith and everything, and he was doing some things he never did back home. But I introduced him to Brad, one of the guys in campus ministry, and they really hit it off." She peeled the wrapper away from the candy bar and offered to break a piece off for Rosemarie, who shook her head. "Anyway, I think he's back on solid ground now; it was like he was drowning for a while."

Rosemarie smiled and dropped her gaze from Cynthia's face to the floor.

"What's wrong?" Cynthia asked, reading her friend's expression.

Rosemarie hesitated, then rolled her eyes and sighed. "It's Jonathan," she said, referring to her boyfriend. "He's really making things hard for me."

"What's he doing?"

CASE STUDY

"He just tries, every chance he gets, to argue with me about God's ways. And sometimes I just don't know how to answer him. I mean, I've really learned a lot from you and the Bible study about, you know, right and wrong and all that stuff, but I can't always explain it to him."

The two friends traded sympathetic looks.

Rosemarie spoke again. "You always seem so sure of yourself and what you believe," she said, fastening her eyes on Cynthia's face.

"Oh, Rosie, I have problems and doubts just like you. I don't have all the answers." She grinned. "I don't even have most of them, just ask my roommate." They exchanged knowing smiles; Cynthia's relationship with Teri was still a struggle. "But I do know where to go for the answers, and I have a personal relationship with the Truth...not just as a concept, but as a real person who lives inside me." Her expression was serious again. "See, Rosie, the truth isn't about rules. It's about a relationship, a relationship with the Son of God who loves me so much He died for me."

Rosemarie's eyes clouded with tears and, without saying a word, she began to cry loudly. Cynthia noticed the curious stares of several people standing nearby, but she dismissed those people from her thoughts and concentrated wholly on Rosemarie. She draped an arm around her friend and guided her to a vinyl seat arrangement nearby.

They sat side by side. Cynthia swallowed hard and whispered to Rosie. "You want Jesus in your life, don't you?"

Rosemarie nodded.

Questions

1. Have you ever felt like Jesse (in the above "Scene on Campus")? Have you ever felt like Rosemarie? Cynthia?

2. Do you know anyone who's in danger of "drowning" in the college environment? How might you be able to help them back to solid ground?

3. Does the revelation of God's truth lead to a relationship with Christ, or must you first have a relationship before you can understand the revelation?

4. If you were Cynthia, how might you proceed in your relationship with Teri? Jesse? Rosemarie?

CASE STUDY

5. If you were Rosemarie, how might you proceed in your relationship with Jonathan?

BIBLE STUDY PASSAGE

bible study passage

A student bows his head in the school cafeteria to pray a silent grace over his cheeseburger and fries. A university professor responds to a direct question by stating her conviction that homosexual behavior is immoral. A mother of four tells a convenience store manager that she is offended by the prominent display of pornographic magazines by the cash register. These individuals, while they may be acting according to their convictions, are liable to be accused of intolerance, even bigotry.

That's because tolerance has arisen in our culture as a new cardinal virtue. It has become synonymous with goodness and open-mindedness; intolerance has come to connote bigotry. Many people think that Christians

Daniel 6:1-23

It pleased Darius to appoint 120 satraps to rule throughout the kingdom, with three administrators over them, one of whom was Daniel. The satraps were made accountable to them so that the king might not suffer loss. Now Daniel so distinguished himself among the administrators and the satraps by his exceptional qualities that the king planned to set him over the whole kingdom. At this, the administrators and the satraps tried to find grounds for charges against Daniel in his conduct of government affairs, but they were unable to do so. They could find no corruption in him, because he was trustworthy and neither corrupt nor negligent. Finally these men said, "We will never find any basis for charges against this man Daniel unless it has something to do with the law of his God."

So the administrators and the satraps went as a group to the king and said: "O King Darius, live for ever! The royal administrators, prefects, satraps, advisers and governors have all agreed that the king should issue an edict and enforce the decree that anyone who prays to any god or man during the next thirty days, except to you, O king, shall be thrown into the lions' den. Now, O king, issue the decree and put it in writing so that it cannot be altered—in accordance with the laws of the Medes and Persians, which cannot be repealed." So King Darius put the decree in writing. 'Now when Daniel learned that the decree had been published, he went home to his upstairs room where the windows opened toward Jerusalem. Three times a day he got down on his knees and prayed, giving thanks to his God, just as he had done before. Then these men went as a group and found Daniel praying and asking God for help. So they went to the king and spoke to him about his royal decree: "Did you not publish a decree that during the next thirty days anyone who prays to any god or man except to you, O king, would be thrown into the lions' den?"

The king answered, "The decree stands—in accordance with the laws of the Medes and Persians, which cannot be repealed."

Then they said to the king, "Daniel, who is one of the exiles from Judah, pays no attention to you, O king, or to the decree you put in writing. He still prays three times a day." When the king heard this, he was greatly distressed; he was determined to rescue Daniel and made every effort until sundown to save him.

Then the men went as a group to the king and said to him, "Remember, O king, that according to the law of the Medes and Persians no decree or edict that the king issues can be changed."

So the king gave the order, and they brought Daniel and threw him into the lions' den. The king said to Daniel, "May your God, whom you serve continually, rescue you!"

A stone was brought and placed over the mouth of the den, and the king sealed it with his own signet ring and with the rings of his nobles, so that Daniel's situation might not be changed. Then the king returned to his palace and spent the night without eating and without any entertainment being brought to him. And he could not sleep.

At the first light of dawn, the king got up and hurried to the lions' den. When he came near the den, he called to Daniel in an anguished voice, "Daniel, servant of the living God, has your God, whom you serve continually, been able to rescue you from the lions?"

Daniel answered, "O king, live forever! My God sent his angel, and he shut the mouths of the lions. They have not hurt me, because I was found innocent in his sight. Nor have I ever done any wrong before you, O king."

The king was overjoyed and gave orders to lift Daniel out of the den. And when Daniel was lifted from the den, no wound was found on him, because he had trusted in his God.

who talk about the truth (about God, Christ, or right and wrong) or pray politely in a public place are displaying intolerance toward those who do not agree with them.

Tolerance can be a good thing. Godly people will give due consideration to people whose practices differ from their own; they will be courteous and kind to those who don't view things the same way they do, refusing to judge anyone unkindly because God is the only one capable of judging righteously (Psalm 9:3-10; Romans 14:10-13).

But the fact that we are not to pass judgment on each other does not change the fact that truth is absolute. It is God's job to judge; it is our job to live according to His truth, and to share that truth in love and compassion.

So how do you do that? It's one thing to talk about biblical truth at church or a campus Bible study, but you are bound to face questions and challenges from professors, from classmates, from the media, and from others. How do you take the truth to the streets? How do you "tell the truth" to those who don't share your convictions? How do you balance absolute truth and appropriate tolerance?

Verse to Remember

"God... wants all men to be saved and to come to a knowledge of the truth" (1 Timothy 2:3-4).

Read

Read Daniel 6:1-23.

Study

1. Verse 4 of the Scriptural account mentions something about Daniel's character and behavior. What does it say? Why is that important for someone who is about to take a stand for truth?

2. Verses 10-16 describe how Daniel took a stand for truth. Which of the following words do you think describe his behavior? (check all that apply, and discuss your response)

❑ obnoxious	❑ resolute
❑ angry	❑ quiet
❑ determined	❑ confident
❑ bitter	❑ unkind
❑ disrespectful	❑ polite
❑ sarcastic	❑ wimpy
❑ haughty	❑ brave
❑ spiteful	❑ embarrassed

3. How did Daniel respond to the news that his beliefs and practices had been banned? (v. 11) Discuss.

4. Do you think his behavior was "intolerant" of the Babylonians' religions and customs? Discuss.

"As important as your obligation as a doctor, a lawyer, or a business leader may be, your human connections with your spouse, your children, and your friends are the most important investment you will ever make. At the end of your life, you will never regret not having passed one more test, not winning one more verdict, or not closing one more deal, but you will regret time not spent with your spouse, your children, or your friends."

— Barbara Bush in a commencement address at Wellesley College (quoted in "Health Fitness," Home Life Dec 1994), 8.

5. Do you think Daniel knew that standing for truth might bring unpleasant consequences?

6. How did Daniel treat the king after surviving a night with the lions (verse 21-22)? (check all that apply)

❑ disrespectfully	❑ angrily
❑ by praising God	❑ apologetically
❑ happily	❑ confidently
❑ bitterly	❑ unkindly
❑ respectfully	❑ politely
❑ sarcastically	❑ haughtily
❑ spitefully	❑ with dignity

7. Read Daniel 6:16-17 and Daniel 6:23-28. Compare the two. What was the immediate effect of Daniel's stand for truth (vv. 16-17)? What was the eventual result (vv. 23-28)?

Apply

apply

• Using the items you checked in the list on page 153 and this page as a guide, what guidelines can you lay down to help you take a Daniel-like stand in a Babylonian-type culture? (For example, you may decide, "When I stand for truth, I will speak respectfully, act kindly...etc.") Compose a set of guidelines as a group and have someone write them down.

Reflect

reflect

• Do you think that kind of behavior will guarantee that you'll never be criticized or accused of being intolerant? Why or why not?

Conclude

"Therefore," Paul wrote, after discussing the kinds of things the Christian is up against in an often-hostile culture, "put on the full armor of God, so that when the day of evil comes, you may be able to **stand** your ground, and after you have done everything, to stand" (Ephesians 6:13). Stand for truth, then, unashamedly telling your family, friends, classmates, and community the truth about right and wrong, about how to make right choices, and about the loving God who longs to protect and provide for all of us.

You can do that with increasing effectiveness if you:

- Practice the 4Cs process for making right choices yourself, relating this biblical process to the moral decisions you face

- Encourage others to give thoughtful consideration to the choices they make (and the consequences that result)

- If your church or campus group has not already done so, encourage the implementation of the total Right From Wrong resources, which includes material for group sessions and workbooks for all age levels, video series' for youth and adults, and many other helpful components (see pages 172-175 for a list of available materials). The Right From Wrong resources will be most helpful and impactful if used in a church-wide emphasis.

- Suggest that your group begin the *Out of the Moral Maze* workbook and group sessions with a new group of students, perhaps giving you and some of your fellow group members an opportunity to lead others through the course.

Pray

Are you equipped to navigate your way out of the moral maze? Are you ready to communicate biblical truth to others? Are you ready to take it to the streets and take a godly stand for truth in your community? If you are, take a moment to close today's study in prayer, perhaps using a form like "Today's Prayer." (on this page)

Today's Prayer

(Read aloud) Dear Father, I praise You because You are the living God and You endure forever. Help me to be like Daniel, who "was trustworthy and neither corrupt nor negligent." Help me to be like Daniel, who stood for truth and trusted You to stand for him. Help me to be like Daniel, who was not ashamed to tell the truth about You and Your commands, even when it meant facing lions. Help me to be like Daniel, who was not afraid to stand alone, who was not afraid to stand for truth, who was not afraid to stand on Your Word, Amen.

Notes from Session Eight

1. I have the following questions...

2. I have the following concerns...

3. Because of this session, I feel...

Here are some very specific strategies that will enable two people who love each other to wait for marriage:

1) Make purity a shared commitment...

2) Talk to each other...

3) Plan your time together...

4) Develop a support group...

5) Pray for each other on a daily basis...

"Love, Sex & the Whole Person: Living with Unfulfilled Desires," by Tim Stafford (Campus Life, September 1992), 56-58.

TEACHING HELPS

OUT OF THE MORAL MAZE TEACHING HELPS

out of the moral maze

teaching helps

out of the moral maze OUT OF THE MORAL MAZE TEACHING HELPS teaching helps

Begin with prayer You have chosen to lead a study of *Out of the Moral Maze,* or you may have been enlisted by someone else. Maybe you're trying to decide if you're the right person to lead a study for your group. No matter how you've come to this point, begin by praying that. God will show you the right decisions to make about your leadership role.

• ***Out of the Moral Maze*** is a serious study covering a variety of topics of interest to college students—decision making, values, honesty, love, sex. More importantly, this workbook is a study of God's Truth, an intense look at who God is and why we should follow His way. Too often, we view God's commands and direction for our lives as rigid rules which are to be obeyed with fear and trembling. We forget that God has designed each one of us as unique creations, made in His image, that He has a plan for us and knows what is best for us. It's not just a matter of wrong or right, nor is it a matter of good and better. God wants what is best for us and His commands are given in order for us to live according to His standards of excellence.

• **This is an easy book** to read; it's user-friendly, clear, and concise. It is not an easy book to work through, however, because it asks the reader to examine his or her own life, decisions, values, and directions. Each person who chooses to be a part of a study of *Out of the Moral Maze* should be prepared to spend some time in introspection and self-evaluation. A casual study of this workbook will benefit anyone who reads it, but to gain the full benefit, one should be prepared to get involved for the next eight weeks.

• **Before you begin, pray** for yourself as leader. Ask God to open up the parts of your life that need serious evaluation and commit yourself to listen for His will in your own life. Pray for understanding and discernment so that you will be prepared to deal with the serious questions college students may ask in discussions of social and moral issues. Pray for sensitivity and compassion for those students who are struggling with painful situations, bad choices, and serious consequences of past actions.

• **Ask God to call out** strong student leaders who will participate in an initial study of *Out of the Moral Maze.* Spend eight weeks with these students and then multiply your efforts with these students serving as co-leaders alongside an adult facilitator. Some students will want to repeat the study and deal more seriously with issues raised in the first cycle. If this is the case, set aside specific times for further discussion and prayer. Encourage each student to find a prayer partner or an accountability partner.

In some situations, you will need to acknowledge that you are not the person to offer counsel or advice. Enlist the help of trained counselors or refer students to appropriate professional help, as needed.

Before the study

Read this book carefully. Read each scripture passage listed and complete each activity for yourself. Become as familiar as you can with the content of each week and begin looking for current examples from news accounts, television, movies, and music so that you can make the group sessions up-to-date and relevant for your students. Particularly make note to read campus publications for examples which bring the study right to your front door.

- **Read Josh McDowell's** *Right from Wrong.* This book is the basis for the workbook series which includes *Out of the Moral Maze. Right from Wrong* will enhance your study and give greater understanding for you as leader. Other helpful resources are listed on pages 172-175.

- **Be sure that you** understand and are conversive about the precept/principle/person concept (see pages 52-71) as well as the 4Cs process (see pages 72-91). These two concepts are key elements in making right choices and understanding how to apply this brief study to everyday life situations.

- **Advertise the study** and selected date. Emphasize the need for eight weeks of participation from each student who decides to participate. The study is structured for eight group sessions with individual assignments after each of the first seven sessions. Students should be aware to the individual work which is a part of this study. Enlist a group of 10-12 students for optimal group experience.

- **Order a workbook for** each participant. Distribute books at the end of the first group session. Encourage students to bring their books to each group session along with pencil, paper, and a Bible. Worksheets for group sessions are part of the text.

- **Secure a comfortable** and quiet meeting room. Students will need space to write easily and talk freely among themselves. Select a room which is conducive to discussion of serious issues without fear of being overheard or exposed.

- **Obtain other equipment** as needed. You may prefer to lead group sessions using overhead cels of certain Scripture passages. If so, prepare these ahead of time and be sure that the projector is working properly. You may want to have a chalkboard or flip chart available for listing answers in group discussions. Whatever teaching methods are most comfortable for you will be easy to adapt in the group sessions.

- **Before each session,** make a poster, banner, or overhead cel to display the week title at the beginning of the session. Make a second poster for the next session and use it at the end of the group time to introduce the next week's topic. Enlist students who are creative and artistic to help with poster and other advertising. Include currents news stories or headlines as appropriate or pull an interesting quote or statistic from the group session to stimulate interest.

- **Set a time for your** first meeting and begin praying for an openness and enthusiasm among the participants.

- **Remember as a leader** you are to be a facilitator and not a lecturer with students.

In Preparation for Group Sessions

1. Attend all of the group sessions. You have probably received this workbook at the first group session. Each week you will need to do all of that week's activities and assignments before the next group session. This is your schedule.

Before Group Session	Complete in your workbook
Introductory Session	Overview and receive workbooks
1	Week 1: Absolute Truth
2	Week 2: An Acceptable Standard
3	Week 3: Precept/Principle/Person
4	Week 4: Discover the 4Cs
5	Week 5: Random Acts of Honesty
6	Week 6: Love Protection
7	Week 7: Handbook for Great Sex
8	Week 8: Directions for the Maze

2. Take your workbook to every group session along with pencil, paper, and your Bible. Your workbook includes the worksheets you will use during the group sessions.

3. Invite others to join you in this study.

Overview of the text

Out of the Moral Maze is organized in eight sessions. This is the order in which you will proceed.

Outline for teaching

This is a suggested outline for each group session. Alter it as needed depending on the week's topic, current events or situations which have occurred on campus, questions from participants, etc.

1. Begin with prayer:

- for participants
- for leader
- for what God wants to teach you in this session
- for clarity of thought
- for strength to follow God's will
- for others who need to participate in a study of *Out of the Moral Maze*
- for decisions which need to be made this week

2. Introduce the week using the information from each chapter which precedes the case study and group Bible study. Summarize the information, use specific suggestions for each week (see pages 165-171), or choose another method which appeals to you. In each week, there are a variety of questions which you can use to begin discussion; there are also interesting quotes and commentary in the narrow columns. These sidebars may offer some of the best introductory material for prompting discussion.

3. In sessions 2-8, ask for comments or questions from the personal studies which students have completed. If there are no questions, be prepared with one or two specific questions from a daily assignment to stimulate discussion. Vary this from week to week by asking students to share one idea or question with another person or in groups of 2-3. In each week, there are questions which ask students to rate themselves on a given scale or to compare themselves to someone in the study. These and other similar questions are good for discussion starters.
The personal Bible studies

are specific and, at times, challenging. Be sure you have reviewed each day's work and be prepared to discuss questions which student have had trouble answering or those which they find confusing.

4. Present the case study from "The Scene on Campus." Summarize the action or ask students to role play (enlist appropriate actors for each week ahead of time). In small groups, discuss the questions listed. Allow time for brief discussion in the larger group.

5. Read the Group Bible Study passage aloud and ask students to find it in their Bibles or workbooks. Lead students through the group study questions and encourage them to write answers in the their workbooks so that they can refer back to them during personal study times.

6. Allow time for additional questions and comments.

7. Introduce the "Application of Truth" and encourage students to do as many of the suggested activities as they can during the week.

Group Session Schedule

Prayer	(5 minutes)
Introduction	(5-7 minutes)
Review of individual study	(7-10 minutes)
Case study	(5-7 minutes)
Bible study	(15-20 minutes)
Additional discussion	(10 minutes, as time allows)
Application of Truth	(2-3 minutes)
Preview of next session	(2-3 minutes)
Prayer	(5 minutes)

8. Preview what the students will discover in the personal studies before the next group session.

9. Ask for prayer requests. If this time gets too lengthy, provide cards for written prayer requests and take them up at the end of each session. (See the sample on page 169.)

10. Close in prayer.

Week 1—Absolute Truth (pps. 10-31)

Discussion suggestions:

• As a group, define these terms: truth, relativism, absolutism.

• List situations and statistics from this week which illustrate the confusion and mixed messages students confront on college campuses today. Add illustrations from your own campus.

• Ask: "Who is to blame for the problem of low morals and personal character in our country today?" Share answers with the group and compare to the answers on page 17.

• Ask for opinions about these incidents: the Spur Posse (p.10), changing grades on the university computer (p.10), cheating on exams (pp.10-11), codes of behavior (p.11). Are similar situations prevalent on your campus? If so, what are some of them?

• Discuss orientation at your campus. What did you like? What did you dislike? Did you feel your views were welcomed? Challenged?

• Discuss areas of personal values (faith, beliefs) which students have found in question by friends, professors, classmates, etc.

Week 2—An Acceptable Standard (pps. 32-51)

• Ask: "How do you decide what's right and what's wrong?"

• List the top ten stress-inducers for students on your campus.

• Post this quote and ask for responses: "Every man is fully satisfied that there is such a thing as truth, or he would not ask any question."

• Which is the more important question: What is right? or Who says what is right?

• Write a life philosophy statement.

• Identify five freedoms students enjoy away from the watchful eyes of parents. Have these changed from year to year during the college experience? Why or why not?

• Name some situations which are right for one person but wrong for someone else. Why are the boundaries or rules different? What part does culture play? What part does tradition play?

Week 3—Precept/Principle/Person (pps. 52-71)

• Ask: "What do you think Jesus would say to the bossy dean?" Add additional people—real or fictional—and discuss what Jesus would say to them in certain situations.

• Make a list of role models or heroes. What qualities are evident in these people? What keeps someone off the list?

• Make a list of the characteristics of God. Ask each person to rate them according to which is most important or most significant in his/her personal view of God. What do the characteristics of God teach us about what God wants for us? What do they teach us about how we ought to live?

• Introduce the Precept/Principle/Person concept (see pages 52-71) and give examples. In small groups, ask students to list one or two additional examples to share with the larger group.

• Ask each student to write a set of his/her own ten commandments. Photocopy the form on the next page or produce your own. Compile a master list and compare it to the biblical list. Note that the Ten Commandments are not the only commands God gives in the Bible, so we can certainly identify a few more "rules to live by."

My personal ten commandments

my personal ten commandments

1.

2.

3.

4.

5.

6.

7.

8.

9.

10.

Week 4—Discover the 4Cs (pps. 72-91)

• Bring a 5-D hidden image poster and ask students to identify the image. Discuss each person's procedure in finding the image. How do those who can't perceive the image feel about this activity? Relate this to those who are seeking a way out of the confusion of determining right from wrong.

• Ask: "Why do you sometimes choose to do what you know is wrong?" (no fear of reprisal, instant gratification, tired of following the rules, didn't think anyone would get hurt, etc.)

• Introduce the 4Cs process and practice it in several decision-making situations.

• Ask for mottoes or ad slogans which support the idea of getting whatever you want, whenever you want. Answers might include: "You deserve a break today." or "The one with the most toys, wins."

• List factors which come into play when you make a decision (parents, teachers, what others will think, what it will cost, etc.)

Week 5—Random Acts of Honesty (pps. 92-109)

• Ask: "What kind of world would we have if everyone were required to be completely honest in all situations?" Working in pairs, ask students to list situations where complete honesty might be less than wonderful. Then list situations where complete honesty would be a better way to go.

• Discuss which is most frustrating: lying, cheating, stealing, other forms of dishonesty.

• Ask for examples from the past week in which a student was treated dishonestly. Discuss how the student felt, what could have been done to prevent the situation, and what could be done to remedy any harm done.

• List common occurrences of dishonest behavior which students encounter regularly. Note the situation in the case study (see page 94).

• Take a brief survey based on the introduction to Group Bible study on page 96. Compare your group to the statistics listed. Why is it so easy to lie to parents, friends, teachers?

• Identify character traits which students value. Is honesty among these traits? Trustworthiness? Loyalty? Discuss what students look for in those they admire or trust. Why are these traits so valuable? Is it because they are in short supply in most people?

Week 6—Love Protection (pps.110-127)

• Make a large graffiti wall and ask students to define love or to write definitions of love they have heard in movies, on television, or in songs.

• Identify types of love and list characteristics of each type (friendship/ agape; romantic/eros; Christian fellowship/ koinonia).

• Discuss the difference between loving someone and being "in love" with someone.

• Review the 4Cs process and apply it to the case study on page 112. What choice does Cynthia have to make and how might she follow the 4Cs? What about Rosemarie? What is God's protection and provision in decisions about love?

• Ask students to share in groups of two or three about situations where they were not treated in a loving manner. How did they feel about such treatment? How would they respond differently now?

Week 7— Handbook for Great Sex (pps.128-147)

• Ask: Is your view of sex based on God's design or on a cultural concept?

• Collect a variety of popular magazines, including newsmagazine. Be sure to include some which are targeted for men, women, and teenagers. Flip through the magazine and note the advertisements and articles. How many in a brief survey are based on sex? What image of sex do you glean from these magazines?

• Make a list of characteristics popular culture suggests you should have in order to have a "good" sex life? (Include images you noted in the magazine survey, if you did that activity.)

• How does popular culture conflict with biblical teaching about sex?

• Do a quick survey of your students, if they are willing to answer questions confidentially. Do not ask specific questions about their sexual activity, but ask questions about what is right and what is wrong with regard to sexual behavior. (Questions are included in personal studies in this week; see page 134-145.)

• List God's standards for sex. Add to the list as you continue this week's group session.

Week 8— Directions for the Maze (pps.148-158)

• Suggest some situations in which students might stand up for their values. Ask students to respond as they believe others on campus would respond to them. (Some are suggested on page 152, such as praying in the cafeteria or confronting a store owner who sells pornographic material.)

• Ask students to share situations from the last few weeks in which they have practiced the 4Cs process.

• Define these terms: *tolerance, understanding, compassion, commitment*. How do they relate to each other? At what point does tolerance become acceptance?

• Discuss this quote: "What one generation tolerates, the next generation accepts." Is that true? Why or why not?

• Ask students to share what they have learned in the past eight weeks. What tools have they developed to help to find direction out of the moral maze?

• Review definitions from Week 1. Would participants define truth in the same terms now after this study? If not, re-define truth.

My prayer card

Name

Campus address

Prayer request

"Can I share this prayer concern with the group?"
• Additional information

"Would you like to talk with me privately?"
• When and where?

My prayer card

Name

Campus address

Prayer request

"Can I share this prayer concern with the group?"
• Additional information

"Would you like to talk with me privately?"
• When and where?

My prayer card

Name

Campus address

Prayer request

"Can I share this prayer concern with the group?"
• Additional information

"Would you like to talk with me privately?"
• When and where?

My prayer card

Name

Campus address

Prayer request

"Can I share this prayer concern with the group?"
• Additional information

"Would you like to talk with me privately?"
• When and where?

BECAUSE OF MY STUDY

Because of my study...

CAMPAIGN 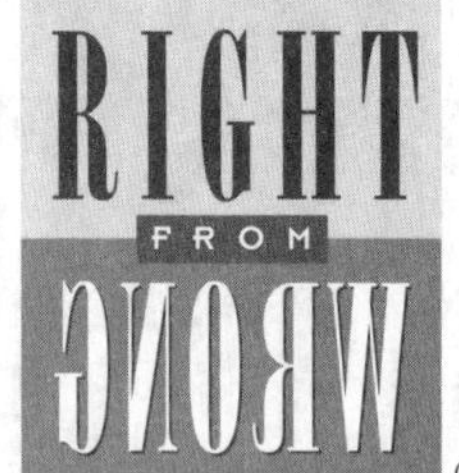

RESOURCES

Passing on the Truth to Our Next Generation

The "Right From Wrong" message, available in numerous formats, provides a blueprint for countering the culture and rebuilding the crumbling foundations of our families.

Read It and Embrace a New Way of Thinking

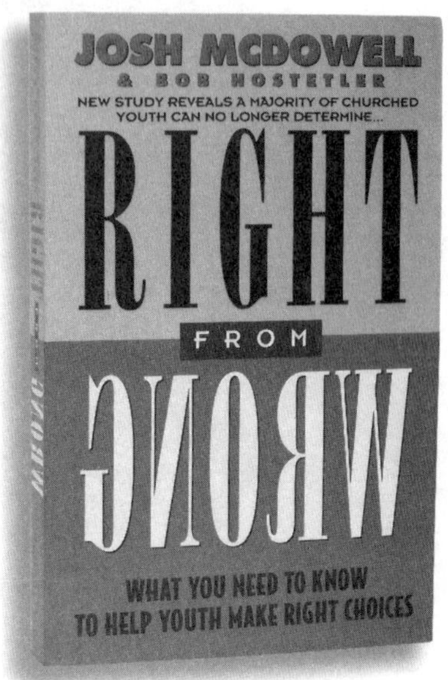

Right From Wrong, Trade Paper Book
ISBN 0-8499-3604-7

The Right From Wrong Book to Adults

Right From Wrong - What You Need to Know to Help Youth Make Right Choices
by Josh McDowell & Bob Hostetler

Our youth no longer live in a culture that teaches an objective standard of right and wrong. Truth has become a matter of taste. Morality has been replaced by individual preference. And today's youth have been affected. Fifty-seven percent (57%) of our churched youth cannot state that an objective standard of right and wrong even exists!

As the centerpiece of the "Right From Wrong" Campaign, this life-changing book provides you with a biblical, yet practical, blueprint for passing on core Christian values to the next generation.

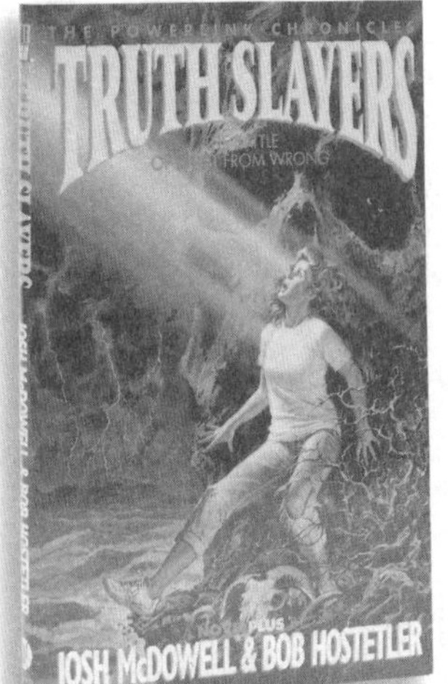

The Truth Slayers, Trade Paper Book
ISBN 0-8499-3662-4

The Truth Slayers Book to Youth

The Truth Slayers - The Battle of Right From Wrong
by Josh McDowell & Bob Hostetler

This book–directed to youth–is written in the popular NovelPlus format and combines the fascinating story of Brittney Marsh, Philip Milford and Jason Withers and the consequences of their wrong choices with Josh McDowell's insights for young adults in sections called "The Inside Story."

The Truth Slayers conveys the critical "Right From Wrong" message that challenges you to rely on God's word as the absolute standard of truth in making right choices.

Hear It and Adopt a New Way of Teaching

Right From Wrong Audio for Adults
by Josh McDowell

What is truth? In three powerful and persuasive talks based on the book *Right From Wrong*, Josh McDowell provides you, your family, and the church with a sound, thorough, biblical, and workable method to clearly understand and defend the truth. Josh explains how to identify absolutes and shows you how to teach youth to determine what is absolutely right from wrong.

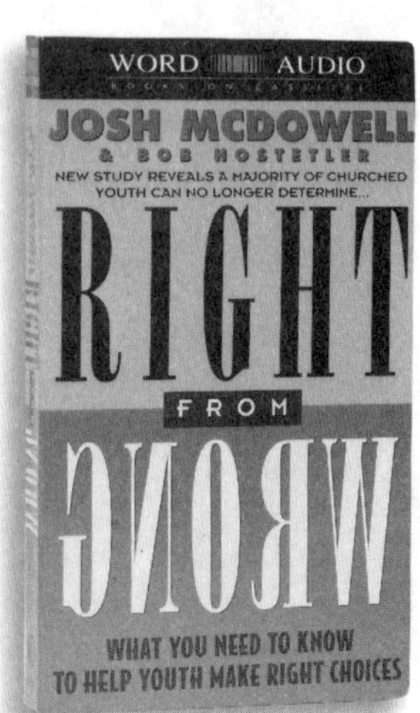

Right From Wrong, Audio–104 min.
ISBN 0-8499-6195-5

CAMPAIGN RIGHT FROM WRONG® RESOURCES

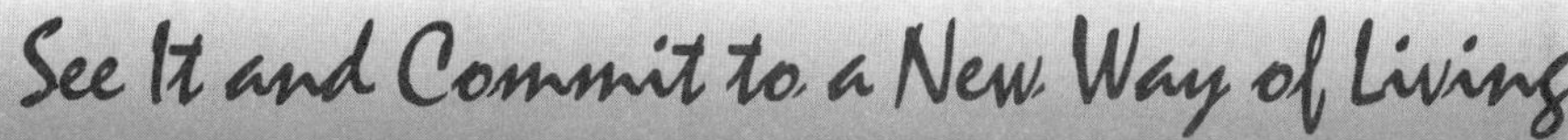

Truth Matters, Adult Video Series
ISBN 0-8499-8587-0

Video Series to Adults

Truth Matters for You and Tomorrow's Generation
Five-part Video Series featuring Josh McDowell

Josh McDowell is at his best in this hard-hitting series that goes beyond surface answers and quick fixes to tackle the real crisis of truth. You will discover the reason for this crisis, and more importantly, how to get you and your family back on track. This series is directed to the entire adult community and is excellent for building momentum in your church to address the loss of values within the family.

This series includes five video sessions, a comprehensive Leader's Guide including samplers from the five "Right From Wrong" Workbooks, the *Right From Wrong* book, the *Truth Slayers* book, and a 12-minute promotional video tape to motivate adults to go through the series.

Video Series to Youth

Setting You Free to Make Right Choices
Five-part Video Series featuring Josh McDowell

Through captivating video illustrations, dynamic teaching sessions, and creative group interaction, this series presents students with convincing evidence that right moral choices must be based on a standard outside of themselves. This powerful course equips your students with the understanding of what is right from what is wrong.

The series includes five video sessions, Leader's Guide with reproducible handout including samplers from the five "Right From Wrong" Workbooks, and the *Truth Slayers* book.

Setting You Free to Make Right Choices, Youth Video Series
ISBN 0-8499-8585-4

CAMPAIGN 

RESOURCES

Practice It and Make Living the Truth a Habit

Workbook for Adults

Truth Matters for You and Tomorrow's Generation
Workbook by Josh McDowell with Leader's Guide

The "Truth Matters" Workbook includes 35 daily activities that help you to instill within your children and youth such biblical values as honesty, love, and sexual purity. By taking just 25 - 30 minutes each day, you will discover a fresh and effective way to teach your family how to make right choices–even in tough situations.

The "Truth Matters" Workbook is designed to be used in eight adult group sessions that encourage interaction and support building. The five daily activities between each group meeting will help you and your family make right choices a habit.

Truth Matters, Member's Workbook ISBN 0-8054-9834-6
Truth Matters, Leader's Guide ISBN 0-8054-9833-8

Workbook for College Students

Out of the Moral Maze
by Josh McDowell with Leader's Instructions

Students entering college face a culture that has lost its belief in absolutes. In today's society, truth is a matter of taste; morality of individual preference. "Out of the Moral Maze" will provide any truth-seeking collegiate with a sound moral guidance system based on God and His Word as the determining factor for making right moral choices.

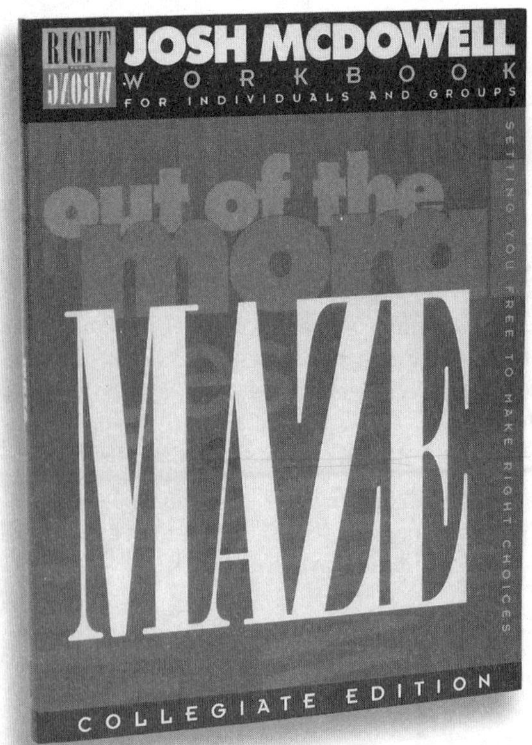

Out of the Moral Maze, Member's Workbook with Leader's Instructions
ISBN 0-8054-9832-X